Apache ZooKeeper Essentials

A fast-paced guide to using Apache ZooKeeper
to coordinate services in distributed systems

Saurav Haloi

BIRMINGHAM - MUMBAI

Apache ZooKeeper Essentials

First published: January 2015

Production reference: 1220115

Published by Packt Publishing Ltd.
Livery Place
35 Livery Street
Birmingham B3 2PB, UK.

ISBN 978-1-78439-132-4

www.packtpub.com

Credits

Author
Saurav Haloi

Reviewers
Hanish Bansal

Christopher Tang, PhD

Commissioning Editor
Ashwin Nair

Acquisition Editor
Richard Harvey

Rebecca Youé

Content Development Editor
Ajinkya Paranjape

Technical Editor
Anushree Arun Tendulkar

Copy Editors
Karuna Narayanan

Alfida Paiva

Project Coordinator
Harshal Ved

Proofreaders
Martin Diver

Ameesha Green

Indexer
Hemangini Bari

Production Coordinator
Melwyn D'sa

Cover Work
Melwyn D'sa

About the Author

Saurav Haloi works as a principal software engineer at EMC in its data protection and availability division. With more than 10 years of experience in software engineering, he has also been associated with prestigious software firms such as Symantec Corporation and Tata Consultancy Services, where he worked in the design and development of complex, large-scale, multiplatform, multi-tier, and enterprise software systems in a storage, networking, and distributed systems domain. He has been using Apache ZooKeeper since 2011 in a variety of different contexts. He graduated from National Institute of Technology, Surathkal, India, with a bachelors degree in computer engineering. An open source enthusiast and a hard rock and heavy metal fanatic, he lives in the city of Pune in India, which is also known as the Oxford of the East.

I would like to thank my family for their support and encouragement throughout the writing of this book.

It was a pleasure to work with Packt Publishing, and I would like to thank everyone associated with this book: the editors, reviewers, and project coordinators, for their valuable comments, suggestions, and assistance during the book development period. Special thanks to Ajinkya Paranjape, my content development editor, who relentlessly helped me while writing this book and patiently answered all my queries relating to the editorial processes.

I would also like to thank the Apache ZooKeeper contributors, committers, and the whole community for developing such a fantastic piece of software and for their continuous effort in getting ZooKeeper to the shape it is in now. Kudos to all of you!

About the Reviewers

Hanish Bansal is a software engineer with over 3 years of experience in developing Big Data applications. He has worked on various technologies such as the Spring framework, Hibernate, Hadoop, Hive, Flume, Kafka, Storm, and NoSQL databases, which include HBase, Cassandra, MongoDB, and SearchEngines such as ElasticSearch. He graduated in Information Technology from Jaipur Engineering College and Research Center, Jaipur, India. He is currently working in Big Data R&D Group in Impetus Infotech Pvt. Ltd., Noida (UP). He published a white paper on how to handle data corruption in ElasticSearch, which can be read at `http://bit.ly/1pQlvy5`. In his spare time, he loves to travel and listen to Punjabi music.

You can read his blog at `http://hanishblogger.blogspot.in/` and follow him on Twitter at `@hanishbansal786`.

> I would like to thank my parents for their love, support, encouragement, and the amazing opportunities they've given me over the years.

Christopher Tang, PhD, is a technologist and software engineer who develops scalable systems for research and analytics-oriented applications that involve rich data in biology, education, and social engagement. He was one of the founding engineers in the Adaptive Learning and Data Science team at Knewton, where Apache ZooKeeper is used with PettingZoo for distributed service discovery and configuration. He has a BS degree in biology from MIT, and received his doctorate degree from Columbia University after completing his thesis in computational protein structure recognition. He currently resides in New York City, where he works at JWPlayer and advises startups such as KnewSchool, FindMine, and Moclos.

> I'd like to extend my thanks to my family for their loving support, without which all these wonderful opportunities would not have been open to me.

www.PacktPub.com

Support files, eBooks, discount offers, and more

For support files and downloads related to your book, please visit www.PacktPub.com.

Did you know that Packt offers eBook versions of every book published, with PDF and ePub files available? You can upgrade to the eBook version at www.PacktPub.com and as a print book customer, you are entitled to a discount on the eBook copy. Get in touch with us at service@packtpub.com for more details.

At www.PacktPub.com, you can also read a collection of free technical articles, sign up for a range of free newsletters and receive exclusive discounts and offers on Packt books and eBooks.

https://www2.packtpub.com/books/subscription/packtlib

Do you need instant solutions to your IT questions? PacktLib is Packt's online digital book library. Here, you can search, access, and read Packt's entire library of books.

Why subscribe?

- Fully searchable across every book published by Packt
- Copy and paste, print, and bookmark content
- On demand and accessible via a web browser

Free access for Packt account holders

If you have an account with Packt at www.PacktPub.com, you can use this to access PacktLib today and view nine entirely free books. Simply use your login credentials for immediate access.

To my parents

Table of Contents

Preface

Architecting and building a distributed system is not a trivial job, and implementing coordination systems for the distributed applications is even harder. They are often prone to errors such as race conditions and deadlocks, and such bugs are not easily detectable. Apache ZooKeeper has been developed with this objective in mind, to simplify the task of developing coordination and synchronization systems from scratch. ZooKeeper is an open source service, which enables high performance and provides highly available coordination services for distributed applications.

Apache ZooKeeper is a centralized service, which exposes a simple set of primitives that distributed applications can build on, in order to implement high-level services such as naming, configuration management, synchronization, group services, and so on. ZooKeeper has been designed to be easily programmable with its simple and elegant set of APIs and client bindings for a plethora of languages.

Apache ZooKeeper Essentials takes readers through an enriching practical journey of learning ZooKeeper and understanding its role in developing scalable and robust distributed applications. It starts with a crisp description of why building coordination services for distributed applications is hard, which lays the stepping stone for the need to know and learn ZooKeeper. This book then describes the installation and configuration of a ZooKeeper instance, after which readers will get a firsthand experience of using it.

This book covers the core concepts of ZooKeeper internals, its administration, and the best practices for its usage. The ZooKeeper APIs and the data model are presented in the most comprehensive manner for both beginners and experts, followed by programming with ZooKeeper. Examples of developing client applications have been given in three languages: Java, C, and Python. A full chapter has been dedicated to discuss the various ZooKeeper recipes so that readers get a vivid understanding of how ZooKeeper can be used to carry out common distributed system tasks.

This book also introduces readers to two projects: Curator and Exhibitor, which are used to ease the use of ZooKeeper in client applications and its management in production. Real-world examples of software projects that use ZooKeeper have been cited for readers to understand how ZooKeeper solves real problems. This is followed by examples of organizations that use ZooKeeper in their production platforms and enterprise software systems.

Apache ZooKeeper Essentials will help readers learn everything they need to get a firm grasp of ZooKeeper so that they can start building scalable and high-performant distributed applications with ease and full confidence.

What this book covers

Chapter 1, A Crash Course in Apache ZooKeeper, introduces you to distributed systems and explains why getting distributed coordination is a hard problem. It then introduces you to Apache ZooKeeper and explains how ZooKeeper solves coordination problems in distributed systems. After this, you will learn how to install and configure ZooKeeper, and get ready to start using it.

Chapter 2, Understanding the Inner Workings of Apache ZooKeeper, discusses the architecture of ZooKeeper and introduces you to its data model and the various operations supported by it. This chapter then delves deeper into the internals of ZooKeeper so that you understand how various components of ZooKeeper function in tandem.

Chapter 3, Programming with Apache ZooKeeper, introduces you to programming with the ZooKeeper client libraries and explains how to develop client applications for ZooKeeper in Java, C, and Python. This chapter presents ready-to-compile code for you to understand the nitty-gritty of ZooKeeper programming.

Chapter 4, Performing Common Distributed System Tasks, discusses the various recipes of distributed system tasks such as locks, queues, leader election, and so on. After going through these recipes, you will understand how ZooKeeper can be used to solve common coordination problems that are often encountered while building distributed systems.

Chapter 5, Administering Apache ZooKeeper, provides you with all the information that you need to know about the administration and configuration of ZooKeeper. It also presents the best practices of ZooKeeper usage and the various ways to monitor it.

Chapter 6, Decorating ZooKeeper with Apache Curator, cites details about two projects, Curator and Exhibitor, that make ZooKeeper programming and management easier and simpler.

Chapter 7, ZooKeeper in Action, discusses examples of real-world software systems, which use ZooKeeper at its core to carry out their functionalities. This chapter also presents examples of how various organizations are using ZooKeeper in their distributed platforms to solve coordination and synchronization problems and to build scalable and highly performant systems.

What you need for this book

Readers who are familiar with the concepts of distributed systems and any high-level programming language such as Java, C, or Python will feel very comfortable to grasp the concepts and code samples presented in this book with much ease. However, the book doesn't need readers to have any prior experience with Apache ZooKeeper.

The procedure to download, install, and configure ZooKeeper is presented in the first chapter of this book. To play around with ZooKeeper and run the example code of this book, readers need to have access to a system with the following requirements:

- **Operating System**: A recent version of a Linux operating system, such as Ubuntu, Fedora, or CentOS.
- **Java SE Development Kit 7**: This is downloadable from Oracle at http://www.oracle.com/technetwork/java/javase/downloads/jdk7-downloads-1880260.html.
- **GCC Compiler suite**: This compiles the C code of this book. GCC usually comes pre-installed with Ubuntu, Fedora flavor, or Linux, or it can be installed as follows:
    - For Ubuntu, the `sudo apt-get install gcc` command is used.
    - For Fedora/CentOS, the `sudo yum install gcc` command can be used.
- **Python 2.7.x**: This is required to run the Python code samples. Python can be downloaded from https://www.python.org/downloads/.

Who this book is for

Apache ZooKeeper Essentials is intended for students, software professionals, and administrators who are involved in the design, implementation, or maintenance of complex distributed applications and platforms. This book will allow both beginners as well as individuals who already have some exposure to ZooKeeper to master the concepts of ZooKeeper, its usage, and programming. Some sections of this book assume that the readers have prior knowledge of the concepts of distributed systems and are familiar with a high-level programming language, but no prior experience with ZooKeeper is required.

Conventions

In this book, you will find a number of styles of text that distinguish between different kinds of information. Here are some examples of these styles, and an explanation of their meaning.

Code words in text are shown as follows: "The `org.apache.zookeeper` is composed of the interface definition for ZooKeeper watches and various callback handlers of ZooKeeper."

A block of code is set as follows:

```
public class HelloZooKeeper {
  public static void main(String[] args) throws IOException {
    String hostPort = "localhost:2181";
    String zpath = "/";
    List <String> zooChildren = new ArrayList <String> ();
    ZooKeeper zk = new ZooKeeper(hostPort, 2000, null);
  }
}
```

When we wish to draw your attention to a particular part of a code block, the relevant lines or items are set in bold:

```
from kazoo.client import KazooClient
zoo_path = '/MyPath'
zk = KazooClient(hosts='localhost:2181')
zk.start()
zk.ensure_path(zoo_path)
```

Any command-line input or output is written as follows:

`${ZK_HOME}/bin/zkCli.sh -server zk_server:port`

New terms and **important words** are shown in bold. Words that you see on the screen, in menus, or dialog boxes for example, appear in the text like this: "The **MBeans** tab shows detailed information about ZooKeeper's internal state."

Warnings or important notes appear in a box like this.

Tips and tricks appear like this.

Reader feedback

Feedback from our readers is always welcome. Let us know what you think about this book—what you liked or disliked. Reader feedback is important for us as it helps us develop titles that you will really get the most out of.

To send us general feedback, simply e-mail feedback@packtpub.com, and mention the book's title in the subject of your message.

If there is a topic that you have expertise in and you are interested in either writing or contributing to a book, see our author guide at www.packtpub.com/authors.

Customer support

Now that you are the proud owner of a Packt book, we have a number of things to help you to get the most from your purchase.

Downloading the example code

You can download the example code files from your account at http://www.packtpub.com for all the Packt Publishing books you have purchased. If you purchased this book elsewhere, you can visit http://www.packtpub.com/books/content/support and register to have the files e-mailed directly to you.

Errata

Although we have taken every care to ensure the accuracy of our content, mistakes do happen. If you find a mistake in one of our books—maybe a mistake in the text or the code—we would be grateful if you could report this to us. By doing so, you can save other readers from frustration and help us improve subsequent versions of this book. If you find any errata, please report them by visiting http://www.packtpub.com/submit-errata, selecting your book, clicking on the **Errata Submission Form** link, and entering the details of your errata. Once your errata are verified, your submission will be accepted and the errata will be uploaded to our website or added to any list of existing errata under the Errata section of that title.

To view the previously submitted errata, go to https://www.packtpub.com/books/content/support and enter the name of the book in the search field. The required information will appear under the **Errata** section.

Piracy

Piracy of copyrighted material on the Internet is an ongoing problem across all media. At Packt, we take the protection of our copyright and licenses very seriously. If you come across any illegal copies of our works in any form on the Internet, please provide us with the location address or website name immediately so that we can pursue a remedy.

Please contact us at `copyright@packtpub.com` with a link to the suspected pirated material.

We appreciate your help in protecting our authors and our ability to bring you valuable content.

Questions

If you have a problem with any aspect of this book, you can contact us at `questions@packtpub.com`, and we will do our best to address the problem.

1

A Crash Course in Apache ZooKeeper

In the past couple of decades, the Internet has changed the way we live our lives. Services offered over the Internet are often backed up by complex software systems, which span over a large number of servers and are often located geographically apart. Such systems are known as distributed systems in computer science terminology. In order to run these large systems correctly and efficiently, processes within these systems should have some sort of agreement among themselves; this agreement is also known as distributed coordination. An agreement by the components that constitute the distributed system includes the overall goal of the distributed system or an agreement to accomplish some subtasks that ultimately lead to the goal. This is not as simple as it sounds, because the processes must not only agree but also know and be sure about what their peers agree to.

Although coordinating tasks and processes in a large distributed system sounds easy, it is a very tough problem when it comes to implementing them correctly in a fault-tolerant manner. Apache ZooKeeper, a project of the Apache Software Foundation, aims to solve these coordination problems in the design and development of distributed systems by providing a set of reliable primitives through simple APIs.

In this chapter, we will cover the following topics:

- What a distributed system is and its characteristics
- Why coordination in a distributed system is hard
- An introduction to Apache ZooKeeper
- Downloading and installing Apache ZooKeeper
- Connecting to ZooKeeper with the ZooKeeper shell
- Multinode ZooKeeper cluster configuration

Defining a distributed system

A distributed system is defined as a software system that is composed of independent computing entities linked together by a computer network whose components communicate and coordinate with each other to achieve a common goal. An e-mail system such as Gmail or Yahoo! Mail is an example of such a distributed system. A multiplayer online game that has the capability of being played by players located geographically apart is another example of a distributed system.

In order to identify a distributed system, here are the key characteristics that you need to look out for:

- **Resource sharing**: This refers to the possibility of using the resources in the system, such as storage space, computing power, data, and services from anywhere, and so on

- **Extendibility**: This refers to the possibility of extending and improving the system incrementally, both from hardware and software perspectives

- **Concurrency**: This refers to the system's capability to be used by multiple users at the same time to accomplish the same task or different tasks

- **Performance and scalability**: This ensures that the response time of the system doesn't degrade as the overall load increases

- **Fault tolerance**: This ensures that the system is always available even if some of the components fail or operate in a degraded mode

- **Abstraction through APIs**: This ensures that the system's individual components are concealed from the end users, revealing only the end services to them

It is difficult to design a distributed system, and it's even harder when a collection of individual computing entities are programmed to function together. Designers and developers often make some assumptions, which are also known as fallacies of distributed computing. A list of these fallacies was initially coined at Sun Microsystems by engineers while working on the initial design of the **Network File System (NFS)**; you can refer to these in the following table:

Assumptions	Reality
The network is reliable	In reality, the network or the interconnection among the components can fail due to internal errors in the system or due to external factors such as power failure.
Latency is zero	Users of a distributed system can connect to it from anywhere in the globe, and it takes time to move data from one place to another. The network's quality of service also influences the latency of an application.

Assumptions	Reality
Bandwidth is infinite	Network bandwidth has improved many folds in the recent past, but this is not uniform across the world. Bandwidth depends on the type of the network (T1, LAN, WAN, mobile network, and so on).
The network is secure	The network is never secure. Often, systems face denial of-service attacks for not taking the security aspects of an application seriously during their design.
Topology doesn't change	In reality, the topology is never constant. Components get removed/added with time, and the system should have the ability to tolerate such changes.
There is one administrator	Distributed systems never function in isolation. They interact with other external systems for their functioning; this can be beyond administrative control.
Transport cost is zero	This is far from being true, as there is cost involved everywhere, from setting up the network to sending network packets from source to destination. The cost can be in the form of CPU cycles spent to actual dollars being paid to network service providers.
The network is homogeneous	A network is composed of a plethora of different entities. Thus, for an application to function correctly, it needs to be interoperable with various components, be it the type of network, operating system, or even the implementation languages.

Distributed system designers have to design the system keeping in mind all the preceding points. Beyond this, the next tricky problem to solve is to make the participating computing entities, or independent programs, coordinate their actions. Often, developers and designers get bogged down while implementing this coordination logic; this results in incorrect and inefficient system design. It is with this motive in mind that Apache ZooKeeper is designed and developed; this enables a highly reliable distributed coordination.

Apache ZooKeeper is an effort to develop a highly scalable, reliable, and robust centralized service to implement coordination in distributed systems that developers can straightaway use in their applications through a very simple interface to a centralized coordination service. It enables application developers to concentrate on the core business logic of their applications and rely entirely on the ZooKeeper service to get the coordination part correct and help them get going with their applications. It simplifies the development process, thus making it more nimble.

With ZooKeeper, developers can implement common distributed coordination tasks, such as the following:

- Configuration management
- Naming service
- Distributed synchronization, such as locks and barriers
- Cluster membership operations, such as detection of node leave/node join

Any distributed application needs these kinds of services one way or another, and implementing them from scratch often leads to bugs that cause the application to behave erratically. Zookeeper mitigates the need to implement coordination and synchronization services in distributed applications from scratch by providing simple and elegant primitives through a rich set of APIs.

Why coordination in a distributed system is so challenging

After getting introduced to Apache ZooKeeper and its role in the design and development of a distributed application, let's drill down deeper into why coordination in a distributed system is a hard problem. Let's take the example of doing configuration management for a distributed application that comprises multiple software components running independently and concurrently, spanning across multiple physical servers. Now, having a master node where the cluster configuration is stored and other worker nodes that download it from this master node and auto configure themselves seems to be a simple and elegant solution. However, this solution suffers from a potential problem of the master node being a single point of failure. Even if we assume that the master node is designed to be fault-tolerant, designing a system where change in the configuration is propagated to all worker nodes dynamically is not straightforward.

Another coordination problem in a distributed system is service discovery. Often, to sustain the load and increase the availability of the application, we add more physical servers to the system. However, we can get the client or worker nodes to know about this change in the cluster memberships and availability of newer machines that host different services in the cluster is something. This needs careful design and implementation of logic in the client application itself.

Scalability improves availability, but it complicates coordination. A horizontally scalable distributed system that spans over hundreds and thousands of physical machines is often prone to failures such as hardware faults, system crashes, communication link failures, and so on. These types of failures don't really follow any pattern, and hence, to handle such failures in the application logic and design the system to be fault-tolerant is truly a difficult problem.

Thus, from what has been noted so far, it's apparent that architecting a distributed system is not so simple. Making correct, fast, and scalable cluster coordination is hard and often prone to errors, thus leading to an overall inconsistency in the cluster. This is where Apache ZooKeeper comes to the rescue as a robust coordination service in the design and development of distributed systems.

Introducing Apache ZooKeeper

Apache ZooKeeper is a software project of the Apache Software Foundation; it provides an open source solution to the various coordination problems in large distributed systems. ZooKeeper was originally developed at Yahoo!

A paper on ZooKeeper, *ZooKeeper: Wait-free Coordination for Internet-scale Systems* by Patrick Hunt and Mahadev Konar from Yahoo! Grid and Flavio P. Junqueira and Benjamin Reed from Yahoo! Research, was published in USENIX ATC 2010. You can access the full paper at http://bit.ly/XWSYiz.

ZooKeeper, as a centralized coordination service, is distributed and highly reliable, running on a cluster of servers called a ZooKeeper ensemble. Distributed consensus, group management, presence protocols, and leader election are implemented by the service so that the applications do not need to reinvent the wheel by implementing them on their own. On top of these, the primitives exposed by ZooKeeper can be used by applications to build much more powerful abstractions to solve a wide variety of problems. We will dive deeper into these concepts in *Chapter 4, Performing Common Distributed System Tasks*.

Apache ZooKeeper is implemented in Java. It ships with C, Java, Perl, and Python client bindings. Community-contributed client libraries are available for a plethora of languages such as Go, Scala, Erlang, and so on.

A full listing of the client bindings for ZooKeeper can be found at https://cwiki.apache.org/confluence/display/ZOOKEEPER/ZKClientBindings.

Apache ZooKeeper is widely used by a large number of organizations, such as Yahoo! Inc., Twitter, Netflix, and Facebook, in their distributed application platforms as a coordination service. We will discuss more about how ZooKeeper is used in the real world in *Chapter 7, ZooKeeper in Action*.

> A detailed listing of organizations and projects using ZooKeeper as a coordination service is available at https://cwiki.apache.org/confluence/display/ZOOKEEPER/PoweredBy.

Getting hands-on with Apache ZooKeeper

In this section, we will show you how to download and install Apache ZooKeeper so that we can start using ZooKeeper straightaway. This section is aimed at developers wanting to get their hands dirty using ZooKeeper for their distributed applications' needs by giving detailed installation and usage instructions. We will start with a single node ZooKeeper installation by getting acquainted with the basic configuration, followed by learning the ZooKeeper shell. Finally, you will be taught how to to set up a multinode ZooKeeper cluster.

Download and installation

ZooKeeper is supported by a wide variety of platforms. GNU/Linux and Oracle Solaris are supported as development and production platforms for both server and client. Windows and Mac OS X are recommended only as development platforms for both server and client.

> In this book, we will assume a GNU-based/Linux-based installation of Apache ZooKeeper for installation and other instructions.

ZooKeeper is implemented in Java and requires Java 6 or later versions to run. While Oracle's version of Java is recommended, OpenJDK should also work fine for the correct functioning of ZooKeeper and many of the code samples in this book.

Oracle's version of Java can be downloaded from http://www.oracle.com/technetwork/java/javase/downloads/index.html.

ZooKeeper runs as a server ensemble known as a ZooKeeper ensemble. In a production cluster, three ZooKeeper servers is the minimum recommended size for an ensemble, and it is recommended that you run them on separate machines. However, you can learn and evaluate ZooKeeper by installing it on a single machine in standalone mode.

 A recent stable ZooKeeper distribution can be downloaded from one of the Apache Download Mirrors (http://bit.ly/1xEl8hA). At the time of writing this book, release 3.4.6 was the latest stable version available.

Downloading

Let's download the stable version from one of the mirrors, say Georgia Tech's Apache download mirror (http://b.gatech.edu/1xElxRb) in the following example:

```
$ wget
http://www.gtlib.gatech.edu/pub/apache/zookeeper/stable/zookeeper-
3.4.6.tar.gz
$ ls -alh zookeeper-3.4.6.tar.gz

-rw-rw-r-- 1 saurav saurav 17M Feb 20  2014 zookeeper-3.4.6.tar.gz
```

Installing

Once we have downloaded the ZooKeeper tarball, installing and setting up a standalone ZooKeeper node is pretty simple and straightforward. Let's extract the compressed tar archive into /usr/share:

```
$ tar -C /usr/share -zxf zookeeper-3.4.6.tar.gz

$ cd /usr/share/zookeeper-3.4.6/

$ ls

bin        CHANGES.txt      contrib      docs       ivy.xml   LICENSE.txt
README_packaging.txt        recipes   zookeeper-3.4.6.jar       zookeeper-
3.4.6.jar.md5

build.xml       conf      dist-maven      ivysettings.xml   lib
NOTICE.txt        README.txt       src       zookeeper-3.4.6.jar.asc
zookeeper-3.4.6.jar.sha1
```

The location where the ZooKeeper archive is extracted in our case, /usr/share/zookeeper-3.4.6, can be exported as ZK_HOME as follows:

```
$ export ZK_HOME=/usr/share/zookeeper-3.4.6
```

Configuration

Once we have extracted the tarball, the next thing is to configure ZooKeeper. The conf folder holds the configuration files for ZooKeeper. ZooKeeper needs a configuration file called zoo.cfg in the conf folder inside the extracted ZooKeeper folder. There is a sample configuration file that contains some of the configuration parameters for reference.

Let's create our configuration file with the following minimal parameters and save it in the conf directory:

```
$ cat conf/zoo.cfg
tickTime=2000
dataDir=/var/lib/zookeeper
clientPort=2181
```

The configuration parameters' meanings are explained here:

- tickTime: This is measured in milliseconds; it is used for session registration and to do regular heartbeats by clients with the ZooKeeper service. The minimum session timeout will be twice the tickTime parameter.

- dataDir: This is the location to store the in-memory state of ZooKeeper; it includes database snapshots and the transaction log of updates to the database. Extracting the ZooKeeper archive won't create this directory, so if this directory doesn't exist in the system, you will need to create it and set writable permission to it.

- clientPort: This is the port that listens for client connections, so it is where the ZooKeeper clients will initiate a connection. The client port can be set to any number, and different servers can be configured to listen on different ports. The default is 2181.

We will learn about the various storage, network, and cluster configuration parameters of ZooKeeper in more detail in *Chapter 5, Administering Apache ZooKeeper*.

As mentioned previously, ZooKeeper needs a Java Runtime Environment for it to work.

 It is assumed that readers already have a working version of Java running in their system where ZooKeeper is being installed and configured.

To see if Java is installed on your system, run the following command:

```
$ java -version
```

If Java is installed and its path is configured properly, then depending on the version and release of Java (Oracle or OpenJDK), the preceding command will show the version of Java and Java Runtime installed on your system. For example, in my system, I have Java 1.7.0.67 installed. So, using the preceding command, this will return the following output in my system:

```
$ java -version
java version "1.7.0_67"
Java(TM) SE Runtime Environment (build 1.7.0_67-b01)
Java HotSpot(TM) 64-Bit Server VM (build 24.65-b04, mixed mode)
```

ZooKeeper needs the JAVA_HOME environment variable to be set correctly. To see if this is set in your system, run the following command:

```
$ echo $JAVA_HOME
```

On my system, JAVA_HOME is set to /usr/java/latest, and hence, I got the following output:

```
$ echo $JAVA_HOME
/usr/java/latest
```

Starting the ZooKeeper server

Now, considering that Java is installed and working properly, let's go ahead and start the ZooKeeper server. All ZooKeeper administration scripts to start/stop the server and invoke the ZooKeeper command shell are shipped along with the archive in the bin folder with the following code:

```
$ pwd
/usr/share/zookeeper-3.4.6/bin
$ ls
README.txt  zkCleanup.sh  zkCli.cmd  zkCli.sh  zkEnv.cmd  zkEnv.sh
zkServer.cmd  zkServer.sh
```

The scripts with the .sh extension are for Unix platforms (GNU/Linux, Mac OS X, and so on), and the scripts with the .cmd extension are for Microsoft Windows operating systems.

To start the ZooKeeper server in a GNU/Linux system, you need to execute the `zkServer.sh` script as follows. This script gives options to start, stop, restart, and see the status of the ZooKeeper server:

```
$ ./zkServer.sh
JMX enabled by default
Using config: /usr/share/zookeeper-3.4.6/bin/../conf/zoo.cfg
Usage: ./zkServer.sh
{start|start-foreground|stop|restart|status|upgrade|print-cmd}
```

To avoid going to the ZooKeeper install directory to run these scripts, you can include it in your PATH variable as follows:

```
export PATH=$PATH:/usr/share/zookeeper-3.4.6/bin
```

Executing `zkServer.sh` with the `start` argument will start the ZooKeeper server. A successful start of the server will show the following output:

```
$ zkServer.sh start
JMX enabled by default
Using config: /usr/share/zookeeper-3.4.6/bin/../conf/zoo.cfg
Starting zookeeper ... STARTED
```

To verify that the ZooKeeper server has started, you can use the following ps command:

```
$ ps -ef | grep zookeeper | grep -v grep | awk '{print $2}'
5511
```

If the `jps` command is installed on your system, you can verify the ZooKeeper server's status as follows:

```
$ which jps
jps is /usr/bin/jps
$ jps
5511 QuorumPeerMain
5565 Jps
```

The ZooKeeper process is listed as QuorumPeerMain. In this case, as reported by `jps`, the ZooKeeper server is running with the 5511 process ID that matches the one reported by the ps command.

The ZooKeeper server's status can be checked with the `zkServer.sh` script as follows:

```
$ zkServer.sh status
JMX enabled by default
Using config: /usr/share/zookeeper-3.4.6/bin/../conf/zoo.cfg
Mode: standalone
```

To stop the server process, you can use the same script with the `stop` argument:

```
$ zkServer.sh stop
JMX enabled by default
Using config: /usr/share/zookeeper-3.4.6/bin/../conf/zoo.cfg
Stopping zookeeper ... STOPPED
```

Checking the status of ZooKeeper when it has stopped or is not running will show the following result:

```
$ zkServer.sh status
JMX enabled by default
Using config: /usr/share/zookeeper-3.4.6/bin/../conf/zoo.cfg
Error contacting service. It is probably not running.
```

Once our ZooKeeper instance is running, the next thing to do is to connect to it. ZooKeeper ships with a default Java-based command-line shell to connect to a ZooKeeper instance. There is a C client as well, which we will discuss in a later section.

Connecting to ZooKeeper with a Java-based shell

To start the Java-based ZooKeeper command-line shell, we simply need to run `zkCli.sh` of the `ZK_HOME/bin` folder with the server IP and port as follows:

```
${ZK_HOME}/bin/zkCli.sh -server zk_server:port
```

In our case, we are running our ZooKeeper server on the same machine, so the ZooKeeper server will be `localhost`, or the loopback address will be `127.0.0.1`. The default port we configured was `2181`:

```
$ zkCli.sh -server localhost:2181
```

As we connect to the running ZooKeeper instance, we will see the output similar to the following one in the terminal (some output is omitted):

```
Connecting to localhost:2181
. . . . . . . . . . . . . .
. . . . . . . . . . . . .
Welcome to ZooKeeper!
JLine support is enabled
. . . . . . . . . . . . . .
WATCHER::
WatchedEvent state:SyncConnected type:None path:null
[zk: localhost:2181(CONNECTED) 0]
```

To see a listing of the commands supported by the ZooKeeper Java shell, you can run the help command in the shell prompt:

```
[zk: localhost:2181(CONNECTED) 0] help
ZooKeeper -server host:port cmd args
    connect host:port
    get path [watch]
    ls path [watch]
    set path data [version]
    rmr path
    delquota [-n|-b] path
    quit
    printwatches on|off
    create [-s] [-e] path data acl
    stat path [watch]
    close
    ls2 path [watch]
    history
    listquota path
    setAcl path acl
    getAcl path
    sync path
    redo cmdno
    addauth scheme auth
    delete path [version]
    setquota -n|-b val path
```

We can execute a few simple commands to get a feel of the command-line interface. Let's start by running the `ls` command, which, as in Unix, is used for listing:

```
[zk: localhost:2181(CONNECTED) 1] ls /
[zookeeper]
```

Now, the `ls` command returned a string called `zookeeper`, which is a znode in the ZooKeeper terminology. Note that we will get introduced to the ZooKeeper data model in the next chapter, *Chapter 2, Understanding the Inner Workings of Apache ZooKeeper*. We can create a znode through the ZooKeeper shell as follows:

To begin with, let's create a `HelloWorld` znode with empty data:

```
[zk: localhost:2181(CONNECTED) 2] create /HelloWorld ""
Created /HelloWorld
[zk: localhost:2181(CONNECTED) 3] ls /
[zookeeper, HelloWorld]
```

We can delete the znode created by issuing the `delete` command as follows:

```
[zk: localhost:2181(CONNECTED) 4] delete /HelloWorld
[zk: localhost:2181(CONNECTED) 5] ls /
[zookeeper]
```

The operations shown here will be clearer as we learn more about the ZooKeeper architecture, its data model, and namespace and internals in the subsequent chapters. We will look at setting up the C language-based command-line shell of the ZooKeeper distribution.

Connecting to ZooKeeper with a C-based shell

ZooKeeper is shipped with a C language-based command-line shell. However, to use this shell, we need to build the C sources in `${ZK_HOME}/src/c`. A GNU/GCC compiler is required to build the sources. To build them, just run the following three commands in the preceding directory:

```
$ ./configure
$ make
$ make install
```

By default, this installs the C client libraries under `/usr/local/lib`. The C client libraries are built for both single-threaded as well as multithreaded libraries. The single-threaded library is suffixed with `_st`, while the multithreaded library is suffixed with `_mt`.

The C-based ZooKeeper shell uses these libraries for its execution. As such, after the preceding build procedure, two executables called `cli_st` and `cli_mt` are also generated in the current folder. These two binaries are the single-threaded and multithreaded command-line shells, respectively. When `cli_mt` is run, we get the following output:

```
$ cli_mt
USAGE cli_mt zookeeper_host_list
[clientid_file|cmd:(ls|ls2|create|od|...)]
Version: ZooKeeper cli (c client) version 3.4.6
```

To connect to our ZooKeeper server instance with this C-based shell, execute the following command in your terminal:

```
$ cli_mt localhost:2181
Watcher SESSION_EVENT state = CONNECTED_STATE
Got a new session id: 0x148b540cc4d0004
```

The C-based ZooKeeper shell also supports multiple commands, such as the Java version. Let's see the available commands under this shell by executing the `help` command:

```
help
  create [+[e|s]] <path>
  delete <path>
  set <path> <data>
  get <path>
  ls <path>
  ls2 <path>
  sync <path>
  exists <path>
  wexists <path>
  myid
  verbose
  addauth <id> <scheme>
  quit
  prefix the command with the character 'a' to run the command
  asynchronously.run the 'verbose' command to toggle verbose logging.
  i.e. 'aget /foo' to get /foo asynchronously
```

We can issue the same set of commands to list the znodes, create a znode, and finally delete it:

```
ls /
time = 3 msec
/: rc = 0
zookeeper
time = 5 msec
create /HelloWorld
Creating [/HelloWorld] node
Watcher CHILD_EVENT state = CONNECTED_STATE for path /
[/HelloWorld]: rc = 0
name = /HelloWorld
ls /
time = 3 msec
/: rc = 0
zookeeper
HelloWorld
time = 3 msec
delete /HelloWorld
Watcher CHILD_EVENT state = CONNECTED_STATE for path /
ls /
time = 3 msec
/: rc = 0
zookeeper
time = 3 msec
```

The format of the C-based ZooKeeper shell output displays the amount of time spent during the command execution as well as the return code (rc). A return code equal to zero denotes successful execution of the command.

The C static and shared libraries that we built earlier and installed in /usr/local/lib are required for ZooKeeper programming for distributed applications written in the C programming language. The Perl and Python client bindings shipped with the ZooKeeper distribution are also based on this C-based interface.

Setting up a multinode ZooKeeper cluster

So far, we have set up a ZooKeeper server instance in standalone mode. A standalone instance is a potential single point of failure. If the ZooKeeper server fails, the whole application that was using the instance for its distributed coordination will fail and stop functioning. Hence, running ZooKeeper in standalone mode is not recommended for production, although for development and evaluation purposes, it serves the need.

In a production environment, ZooKeeper should be run on multiple servers in a replicated mode, also called a ZooKeeper ensemble. The minimum recommended number of servers is three, and five is the most common in a production environment. The replicated group of servers in the same application domain is called a **quorum**. In this mode, the ZooKeeper server instance runs on multiple different machines, and all servers in the quorum have copies of the same configuration file. In a quorum, ZooKeeper instances run in a leader/follower format. One of the instances is elected the leader, and others become followers. If the leader fails, a new leader election happens, and another running instance is made the leader. However, these intricacies are fully hidden from applications using ZooKeeper and from developers.

The ZooKeeper configuration file for a multinode mode is similar to the one we used for a single instance mode, except for a few entries. An example configuration file is shown here:

```
tickTime=2000
dataDir=/var/lib/zookeeper
clientPort=2181
initLimit=5
syncLimit=2
server.1=zoo1:2888:3888
server.2=zoo2:2888:3888
server.3=zoo3:2888:3888
```

The two configuration parameters are also explained here:

- initLimit: This parameter is the timeout, specified in number of ticks, for a follower to initially connect to a leader
- syncLimit: This is the timeout, specified in number of ticks, for a follower to sync with a leader

Both of these timeouts are specified in the unit of time called `tickTime`. Thus, in our example, the timeout for `initLimit` is 5 ticks at 2000 milliseconds a tick, or 10 seconds.

The other three entries in the preceding example in the `server.id=host:port:port` format are the list of servers that constitute the quorum. The `.id` identifier is a number that is used for the server with a hostname in the quorum. In our example configuration, the `zoo1` quorum member host is assigned an identifier 1.

The identifier is needed to be specified in a file called `myid` in the data directory of that server. It's important that the `myid` file should consist of a single line that contains only the text (ASCII) of that server's ID. The id must be unique within the ensemble and should have a value between 1 and 255.

Again, we have the two port numbers after each server hostname: 2888 and 3888. They are explained here:

- The first port, 2888, is mostly used for peer-to-peer communication in the quorum, such as to connect followers to leaders. A follower opens a TCP connection to the leader using this port.

- The second port, 3888, is used for leader election, in case a new leader arises in the quorum. As all communication happens over TCP, a second port is required to respond to leader election inside the quorum.

Starting the server instances

After setting up the configuration file for each of the servers in the quorum, we need to start the ZooKeeper server instances. The procedure is the same as for standalone mode. We have to connect to each of the machines and execute the following command:

```
${ZK_HOME}/bin/zkServer.sh start
```

Once the instances are started successfully, we will execute the following command on each of the machines to check the instance states:

```
${ZK_HOME}/bin/zkServer.sh status
```

For example, take a look at the next quorum:

```
[zoo1] # ${ZK_HOME}/bin/zkServer.sh status
JMX enabled by default
Using config: /usr/share/zookeeper-3.4.6/bin/../conf/zoo.cfg
Mode: follower
[zoo2] # ${ZK_HOME}/bin/zkServer.sh status
```

```
JMX enabled by default
Using config: /usr/share/zookeeper-3.4.6/bin/../conf/zoo.cfg
Mode: leader
[zoo3] # ${ZK_HOME}/bin/zkServer.sh status
JMX enabled by default
Using config: /usr/share/zookeeper-3.4.6/bin/../conf/zoo.cfg
Mode: follower
```

As seen in the preceding example, `zoo2` is made the leader of the quorum, while `zoo1` and `zoo3` are the followers. Connecting to the ZooKeeper quorum through the command-line shell is also the same as in standalone mode, except that we should now specify a connection string in the host1:port2, host2:port2 … format to the server argument of `${ZK_HOME}/bin/zkCli.sh`:

```
$ zkCli.sh -server zoo1:2181,zoo2:2181,zoo3:2181
Connecting to zoo1:2181, zoo2:2181, zoo3:2181

... ... ... ...

Welcome to ZooKeeper!

... ... ... ...

[zk: zoo1:2181,zoo2:2181,zoo3:2181 (CONNECTED) 0]
```

Once the ZooKeeper cluster is up and running, there are ways to monitor it using **Java Management Extensions (JMX)** and by sending some commands over the client port, also known as the **Four Letter Words**. We will discuss ZooKeeper monitoring in more detail in *Chapter 5, Administering Apache ZooKeeper*.

Running multiple node modes for ZooKeeper

It is also possible to run ZooKeeper in multiple node modes on a single machine. This is useful for testing purposes. To run multinode modes on the same machine, we need to tweak the configuration a bit; for example, we can set the server name as `localhost` and specify the unique quorum and leader election ports.

Let's use the following configuration file to set up a multinode ZooKeeper cluster using a single machine:

```
tickTime=2000
initLimit=5
syncLimit=2
dataDir=/var/lib/zookeeper
clientPort=2181
server.1=localhost:2666:3666
```

```
server.2=localhost:2667:3667
server.3=localhost:2668:3668
```

As already explained in the previous section, each entry of the server *X* specifies the address and port numbers used by the *X* ZooKeeper server. The first field is the hostname or IP address of server *X*. The second and third fields are the TCP port numbers used for quorum communication and leader election, respectively. As we are starting three ZooKeeper server instances on the same machine, we need to use different port numbers for each of the server entries.

Second, as we are running more than one ZooKeeper server process on the same machine, we need to have different client ports for each of the instances.

Last but not least, we have to customize the dataDir parameter as well for each of the instances we are running.

Putting all these together, for a three-instance ZooKeeper cluster, we will create three different configuration files. We will call these zoo1.cfg, zoo2.cfg, and zoo3.cfg and store them in the conf folder of ${ZK_HOME}. We will create three different data folders for the instances, say zoo1, zoo2, and zoo3, in /var/lib/zookeeper. Thus, the three configuration files are shown next.

Here, you will see the configuration file for the first instance:

```
tickTime=2000
initLimit=5
syncLimit=2
dataDir=/var/lib/zookeeper/zoo1
clientPort=2181
server.1=localhost:2666:3666
server.2=localhost:2667:3667
server.3=localhost:2668:3668
```

The second instance is shown here:

```
tickTime=2000
initLimit=5
syncLimit=2
dataDir=/var/lib/zookeeper/zoo2
clientPort=2182
server.1=localhost:2666:3666
server.2=localhost:2667:3667
server.3=localhost:2668:3668
```

The third and final instance is then shown here:

```
tickTime=2000
initLimit=5
syncLimit=2
dataDir=/var/lib/zookeeper/zoo3
clientPort=2183
server.1=localhost:2666:3666
server.2=localhost:2667:3667
server.3=localhost:2668:3668
```

We also need to fix the server ID parameter correctly in the `myid` file for each instance. This can be done using the following three commands:

```
$ echo 1 > /var/lib/zookeeper/zoo1/myid
$ echo 2 > /var/lib/zookeeper/zoo2/myid
$ echo 3 > /var/lib/zookeeper/zoo3/myid
```

Now, we are all set to start the ZooKeeper instances. Let's start the instances as follows:

```
$ ${ZK_HOME}/bin/zkServer.sh start ${ZK_HOME}/conf/zoo1.cfg
$ ${ZK_HOME}/bin/zkServer.sh start ${ZK_HOME}/conf/zoo2.cfg
$ ${ZK_HOME}/bin/zkServer.sh start ${ZK_HOME}/conf/zoo3.cfg
```

Once all the instances start, we can use the `zkCli.sh` script to connect to the multinode ZooKeeper cluster, like we did earlier:

```
$ ${ZK_HOME}/bin/zkCli.sh -server \
        localhost:2181, localhost:2182, localhost:2183
```

Voila! We have a three-node ZooKeeper cluster running on the same machine!

Summary

In this chapter, you learned the general definition of a distributed system and why coordination among entities that constitute a large system is hard and a very important problem to be solved. You learned how Apache ZooKeeper is a great tool for distributed system designer and developers to solve coordination problems. This chapter provided details on installing and configuring a ZooKeeper in various modes, such as standalone, clustered, and also talked about how to connect to a ZooKeeper service from the command line with the ZooKeeper shell.

In the next chapter, you will learn about the internals and architecture of Apache ZooKeeper. You will learn in detail about the ZooKeeper data model and the API interfaces exposed by the ZooKeeper service. The concepts introduced in the next chapter will help you master the design semantics of ZooKeeper and equip readers with confidence in using ZooKeeper in their distributed applications.

2
Understanding the Inner Workings of Apache ZooKeeper

In the previous chapter, we learned about the general definition of a distributed system and why implementing coordination among components of such a system is hard. We learned how Apache ZooKeeper solves this problem, followed by how to install and configure it. In this chapter, we will read more about the internals and architecture of ZooKeeper. As such, we will cover the following topics here in this second chapter:

- The architecture of the ZooKeeper service
- The data model behind ZooKeeper
- The operations supported by the ZooKeeper data model
- Probing the inner workings of ZooKeeper

A top-down view of the ZooKeeper service

As you are aware, Apache ZooKeeper is a coordination service for distributed applications. It aims to solve the tough problems associated with the coordination of components in a distributed application. It does this by exposing a simple yet powerful interface of primitives. Applications can be designed on these primitives implemented through ZooKeeper APIs to solve the problems of distributed synchronization, cluster configuration management, group membership, and so on.

ZooKeeper is, in itself, a replicated and distributed application, with the intention to be run as a service, similar to the way we run DNS or any other centralized service. A view of the ZooKeeper service is shown in the following diagram:

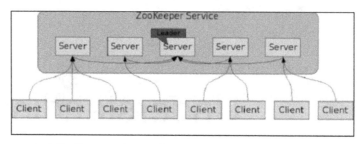

A ZooKeeper service and how clients connect to the service

From the preceding diagram (the image is referenced from `http://zookeeper.apache.org/doc/r3.4.6/zookeeperOver.html`), you will see the replicated set of servers on which the ZooKeeper service is run. This is called an ensemble. Clients can connect to a ZooKeeper service by connecting to any member of the ensemble. You can send and receive requests and responses as well as event notifications between clients and the service, which are all done by maintaining a TCP connection and by periodically sending heartbeats.

> The members of the ensemble are aware of each other's state. By this, I mean that the current in-memory state, transaction logs, and the point-in-time copies of the state of the service are stored in a durable manner in the local data store by the individual hosts that form the ensemble. It is important to remember that ZooKeeper is a highly available service, so as long as a majority of the servers are available, the service will always be available.

With this, ZooKeeper maintains a strict ordering of its transactions, which enables the implementation of advanced distributed synchronization primitives that are simple and reliable. With its design to be robust, reliable, high performing, and fast, this coordination service makes it possible to be used in large and complex distributed applications.

The ZooKeeper data model

As defined by the ZooKeeper wiki, ZooKeeper allows distributed processes to coordinate with each other through a shared hierarchical namespace of data registers. The namespace looks quite similar to a Unix filesystem. The data registers are known as **znodes** in the ZooKeeper nomenclature. You can see examples of znodes in the following image:

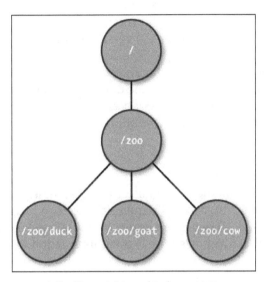

A ZooKeeper's hierarchical namespace

Here, you can see that znodes are organized hierarchically, much like a tree, as a standard filesystem. Some important points to take note of are as follows:

- The root node has one child znode called **/zoo**, which in turn has three znodes.
- Every znode in the ZooKeeper tree is identified by a path, and the path elements are separated by **/**.
- The znodes are called data registers because they can store data. Thus, a znode can have children as well as data associated with it. It's analogous to having a filesystem that allows a file to also be a path.

The data in a znode is typically stored in a byte format, with a maximum data size in each znode of no more than 1 MB. ZooKeeper is designed for coordination, and almost all forms of coordination data are relatively small in size; hence, this limit on the size of data is imposed. It is recommended that the actual data size be much less than this limit as well.

The slash-separated znode paths are canonical and have to be absolute. Relative paths and references are not recognized by ZooKeeper. It is useful to know that the znode names can be composed of Unicode characters and that the znodes can have any name. The exception to this is that the word ZooKeeper is reserved. On top of this, the use of "." is illegal as a path component.

Like files in a filesystem, znodes maintain a stat structure that includes version numbers for data changes and an access control list that changes along with timestamps associated with changes. The version number increases whenever the znode's data changes. ZooKeeper uses the version numbers along with the associated timestamps to validate its in-core cache. The znode version number also enables the client to update or delete a particular znode through ZooKeeper APIs. If the version number specified doesn't match the current version of a znode, the operation fails. However, this can be overridden by specifying 0 as the version number while performing a znode update or delete operation.

Types of znodes

ZooKeeper has two types of znodes: persistent and ephemeral. There is a third type that you might have heard of, called a sequential znode, which is a kind of a qualifier for the other two types. Both persistent and ephemeral znodes can be sequential znodes as well. Note that a znode's type is set at its creation time.

The persistent znode

As the name suggests, persistent znodes have a lifetime in the ZooKeeper's namespace until they're explicitly deleted. A znode can be deleted by calling the `delete` API call. It's not necessary that only the client that created a persistent znode has to delete it. Note that any authorized client of the ZooKeeper service can delete a znode.

It's time to put this newly acquired knowledge into practice, so let's create a persistent znode using the ZooKeeper Java shell:

```
[zk: localhost(CONNECTED) 1] create /[PacktPub] "ApacheZooKeeper"
Created /[PacktPub]
[zk: localhost(CONNECTED) 2] get /[PacktPub]

"ApacheZooKeeper"
```

Persistent znodes are useful for storing data that needs to be highly available and accessible by all the components of a distributed application. For example, an application can store the configuration data in a persistent znode. The data as well as the znode will exist even if the creator client dies.

The ephemeral znode

By contrast, an ephemeral znode is deleted by the ZooKeeper service when the creating client's session ends. An end to a client's session can happen because of disconnection due to a client crash or explicit termination of the connection. Even though ephemeral nodes are tied to a client session, they are visible to all clients, depending on the configured **Access Control List (ACL)** policy.

An ephemeral znode can also be explicitly deleted by the creator client or any other authorized client by using the `delete` API call. An ephemeral znode ceases to exist once its creator client's session with the ZooKeeper service ends. Hence, in the current version of ZooKeeper, ephemeral znodes are not allowed to have children.

To create an ephemeral znode using the ZooKeeper Java Shell, we have to specify the `-e` flag in the `create` command, which can be done using the following command:

```
[zk: localhost(CONNECTED) 1] create -e /[PacktPub] "ApacheZooKeeper"
Created /[PacktPub]
```

Now, since an ephemeral znode is not allowed to have children, if we try to create a child znode to the one we just created, we will be thrown an error, as follows:

```
[zk: localhost(CONNECTED) 2] create -e /[PacktPub]/EphemeralChild
"ChildOfEphemeralZnode"
Ephemerals cannot have children: /[PacktPub]/EphemeralChild
```

The concept of ephemeral znodes can be used to build distributed applications where the components need to know the state of the other constituent components or resources. For example, a distributed group membership service can be implemented by using ephemeral znodes. The property of ephemeral nodes getting deleted when the creator client's session ends can be used as an analogue of a node that is joining or leaving a distributed cluster. Using the membership service, any node is able discover the members of the group at any particular time. We will discuss this in more detail in *Chapter 4, Performing Common Distributed System Tasks*.

The sequential znode

A sequential znode is assigned a sequence number by ZooKeeper as a part of its name during its creation. The value of a monotonously increasing counter (maintained by the parent znode) is appended to the name of the znode.

The counter used to store the sequence number is a signed integer (4 bytes). It has a format of 10 digits with 0 (zero) padding. For example, look at `/path/to/znode-0000000001`. This naming convention is useful to sort the sequential znodes by the value assigned to them.

Sequential znodes can be used for the implementation of a distributed global queue, as sequence numbers can impose a global ordering. They may also be used to design a lock service for a distributed application. The recipes for a distributed queue and lock service will be discussed in *Chapter 4, Performing Common Distributed System Tasks.*

Since both persistent and ephemeral znodes can be sequential znodes, we have a total of four modes of znodes:

- persistent
- ephemeral
- persistent_sequential
- ephemeral_sequential

To create a sequential znode using the ZooKeeper Java shell, we have to use the -s flag of the create command:

```
[zk: localhost(CONNECTED) 1] create -s /[PacktPub]
"PersistentSequentialZnode"
Created /[PacktPub]0000000001

[zk: localhost(CONNECTED) 3] create -s -e /[PacktPub]
"EphemeralSequentialZnode"
Created /[PacktPub]0000000008
```

Keeping an eye on znode changes – ZooKeeper Watches

ZooKeeper is designed to be a scalable and robust centralized service for very large distributed applications. A common design anti-pattern associated while accessing such services by clients is through polling or a pull kind of model. A pull model often suffers from scalability problems when implemented in large and complex distributed systems. To solve this problem, ZooKeeper designers implemented a mechanism where clients can get notifications from the ZooKeeper service instead of polling for events. This resembles a push model, where notifications are pushed to the registered clients of the ZooKeeper service.

Clients can register with the ZooKeeper service for any changes associated with a znode. This registration is known as setting a watch on a znode in ZooKeeper terminology. Watches allow clients to get notifications when a znode changes in any way. A watch is a one-time operation, which means that it triggers only one notification. To continue receiving notifications over time, the client must reregister the watch upon receiving each event notification.

Let's walk through an example of a cluster group membership model to illustrate the concept of ZooKeeper watches and notifications:

- In the cluster, a node, say **Client1**, is interested in getting notified when another node joins the cluster. Any node that is joining the cluster creates an ephemeral node in the ZooKeeper path **/Members**.

- Now, another node, **Client2**, joins the cluster and creates an ephemeral node called **Host2** in **/Members**.

- **Client1** issues a **getChildren** request on the ZooKeeper path **/Members**, and sets a watch on it for any changes. When **Client2** creates a znode as **/Members/Host2**, the watch gets triggered and **Client1** receives a notification from the ZooKeeper service. If **Client1** now issues **getChildren** request on the ZooKeeper path **/Members**, it sees the new znode **Host2**. This flow of the setting of watches, and notifications and subsequent resetting of the watches is shown in the following image:

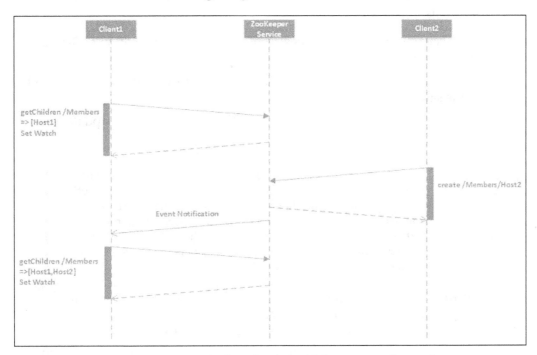

An image to representing how the relationship between two clients and
ZooKeeper works through watches and notifications

ZooKeeper watches are a one-time trigger. What this means is that if a client receives a watch event and wants to get notified of future changes, it must set another watch. Whenever a watch is triggered, a notification is dispatched to the client that had set the watch. Watches are maintained in the ZooKeeper server to which a client is connected, and this makes it a fast and lean method of event notification.

The watches are triggered for the following three changes to a znode:

1. Any changes to the data of a znode, such as when new data is written to the znode's data field using the `setData` operation.

2. Any changes to the children of a znode. For instance, children of a znode are deleted with the `delete` operation.

3. A znode being created or deleted, which could happen in the event that a new znode is added to a path or an existing one is deleted.

Again, ZooKeeper asserts the following guarantees with respect to watches and notifications:

*   ZooKeeper ensures that watches are always ordered in the **first in first out (FIFO)** manner and that notifications are always dispatched in order

*   Watch notifications are delivered to a client before any other change is made to the same znode

*   The order of the watch events are ordered with respect to the updates seen by the ZooKeeper service

> Since ZooKeeper watches are one-time triggers and due to the latency involved between getting a watch event and resetting of the watch, it's possible that a client might lose changes done to a znode during this interval. In a distributed application in which a znode changes multiple times between the dispatch of an event and resetting the watch for events, developers must be careful to handle such situations in the application logic.

When a client gets disconnected from the ZooKeeper server, it doesn't receive any watches until the connection is re-established. If the client then reconnects, any previously registered watches will also be reregistered and triggered. If the client connects to a new server, the watch will be triggered for any session events. This disconnection from a server and reconnection to a new server happens in a transparent way for the client applications.

Although ZooKeeper guarantees that all registered watches get dispatched to the client, even if the client disconnects from one server and reconnects to another server within the ZooKeeper service, there is one possible scenario worth mentioning where a watch might be missed by a client. This specific scenario is when a client has set a watch for the existence of a znode that has not yet been created. In this case, a watch event will be missed if the znode is created, and deleted while the client is in the disconnected state.

The ZooKeeper operations

ZooKeeper's data model and its API support the following nine basic operations:

Operation	Description
create	Creates a znode in a specified path of the ZooKeeper namespace
delete	Deletes a znode from a specified path of the ZooKeeper namespace
exists	Checks if a znode exists in the path
getChildren	Gets a list of children of a znode
getData	Gets the data associated with a znode
setData	Sets/writes data into the data field of a znode
getACL	Gets the **ACL** of a znode
setACL	Sets the **ACL** in a znode
sync	Synchronizes a client's view of a znode with ZooKeeper

Let's look at the ZooKeeper operations mentioned in the preceding table using ZooKeeper Java shell:

1. Create a znode called root with ThisIsTheRootNode as its data:

   ```
   [zk: localhost(CONNECTED) 0] create /root "ThisIsTheRootNode"
   Created /root
   ```

2. Get the content of the just created znode root:

   ```
   [zk: localhost(CONNECTED) 1] get /root
   "ThisIsTheRootNode"
   ...... ......
   ...... ......
   ```

3. Create a child znode `child-1` for root with `ThisIsChild-1` as its data:

```
[zk: localhost(CONNECTED) 2] create /root/child-1
  "ThisIsChild-1"
Created /root/child-1
```

4. Create a child znode `child-2` for root with `ThisIsChild-2` as its data:

```
[zk: localhost(CONNECTED) 3] create /root/child-2
  "ThisIsChild-2"
Created /root/child-2
```

5. List the children of root:

```
[zk: localhost(CONNECTED) 4] ls /root
[child-2, child-1]
```

6. Get the access control listing for root:

```
[zk: localhost(CONNECTED) 5] getAcl /root
'world,'anyone
: cdrwa
```

7. Deleting the root is not allowed as root has 2 child znodes:

```
[zk: localhost(CONNECTED) 6] delete /root
Node not empty: /root
```

8. Delete `child-1`:

```
[zk: localhost(CONNECTED) 7] delete /root/child-1
```

9. Delete `child-2`:

```
[zk: localhost(CONNECTED) 8] delete /root/child-2
```

10. List the content of root:

```
[zk: localhost(CONNECTED) 9] ls2 /root
[]
...... ......
...... ......
```

11. Delete `root`:

```
[zk: localhost(CONNECTED) 10] delete /root
```

Apart from the operations described so far, ZooKeeper also supports batch updates to znodes with an operation called **multi**. This batches together multiple primitive operations into a single unit. A multi operation is also atomic in nature, which means that either all the updates succeed or the whole bunch of updates fails in its entirety.

ZooKeeper does not allow partial writes or reads of the znode data. When setting the data of a znode or reading it, the content of the znode is replaced or read entirely. Update operations in ZooKeeper, such as a `delete` or `setData` operation, have to specify the version number of the znode that is being updated. The version number can be obtained by using the `exists()` call. The `update` operation will fail if the specified version number does not match the one in the znode. Also, another important thing to note is that updates in ZooKeeper are non-blocking operations.

The `read` and `write` operations in ZooKeeper are shown in the following image:

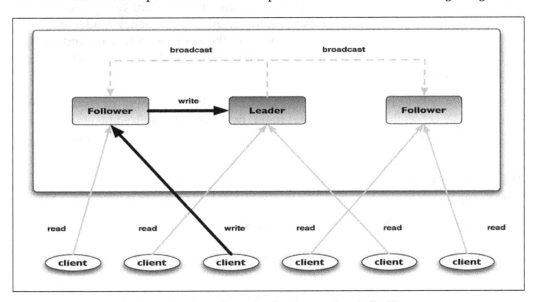

An image that shows the read and write operations in ZooKeeper

From the preceding image, we need to take note of the following two crucial aspects of these operations:

- **Read requests**: These are processed locally in the ZooKeeper server to which the client is currently connected

- **Write requests**: These are forwarded to the leader and go through majority consensus before a response is generated

> The read and write processing by ZooKeeper is described in more detail in the ZooKeeper implementation section later in this chapter.

Watches and ZooKeeper operations

The `write` operations in ZooKeeper are atomic and durable. There is the guarantee of a successful `write` operation if it has been written to persistent storage on a majority of ZooKeeper's servers. However, the eventual consistency model of ZooKeeper permits reads to log the latest state of the ZooKeeper service, and the `sync` operation allows a client to be up-to-date with the most recent state of the ZooKeeper service.

The `read` operations in znodes, such as `exists`, `getChildren`, and `getData`, allow watches to be set on them. On the other hand, the watches triggered by znode's `write` operations, such as `create`, `delete`, and `setData` ACL operations do not participate in watches.

The following are the types of watch events that might occur during a znode state change:

- `NodeChildrenChanged`: A znode's child is created or deleted

- `NodeCreated`: A znode is created in a ZooKeeper path

- `NodeDataChanged`: The data associated with a znode is updated

- `NodeDeleted`: A znode is deleted in a ZooKeeper path

A watch event's type depends on the watch and the operation that triggered it. Some crucial information about how the three main operations have event-generating actions is shown in this table:

Operation	Event-generating Actions
`exists`	A znode is created or deleted, or its data is updated
`getChildren`	A child of a znode is created or deleted, or the znode itself is deleted
`getData`	A znode is deleted or its data is updated

A `watch` event includes the path of the znode where the event was generated. Thus, a client can find a znode creation and deletion for the `NodeCreated` and `NodeDeleted` events through the inspection of the path to the znode. To discover which children have changed after a `NodeChildrenChanged` event, the operation `getChildren` has to be called to retrieve the new list of children. Similarly, in order to discover the new data for a `NodeDataChanged` event, `getData` has to be called.

ZooKeeper provides a set of guarantees from its data model perspectives and watch infrastructure built on top of it, which enables the easy, fast, and scalable building of other distributed coordination primitives:

- **Sequential consistency**: This ensures that the updates from clients are always applied in a FIFO order.
- **Atomicity**: This ensures that the updates either succeed or fail, so there is no partial commit.
- **Single system image**: A client sees the same view of the ZooKeeper service, which doesn't depend on which ZooKeeper server in the ensemble it connects to.
- **Reliability**: This ensures that the updates will persist once they are applied. This is until they are overwritten by some clients.
- **Timeliness**: The clients' view of the system is guaranteed to be up-to-date within a certain time bound. This is known as eventual consistency.

The ZooKeeper access control lists

ZooKeeper's data model provides a mechanism to control the access to znodes using ACL. While creating a znode, the ACLs determine the permissions with respect to the various operations that you can perform on the znodes. The ZooKeeper ACL model is similar to the Unix/Linux file permissions in terms of permitting or preventing operations being done on a znode by setting/unsetting permission bits. However, the ZooKeeper node doesn't have the concept of ownership, which is present in the Unix/Linux filesystem. ACLs are determined on the basis of the authentication mechanism of the client and the ZooKeeper service.

ZooKeeper provides the following built-in authentication mechanisms based on ACLs:

- **World**: This represents anyone who is connecting to the ZooKeeper service
- **Auth**: This represents any authenticated user, but doesn't use any ID
- **Digest**: This represents the username and password way of authentication
- **IP address**: This represents authentication with the IP address of the client

In addition to the authentication schemes mentioned in the preceding list, ZooKeeper also supports a pluggable authentication mechanism, which makes it possible to integrate third-party authentication schemes if needed. Any authentication schemes in ZooKeeper consist of the following two main authentication operations:

- Firstly, the authentication framework in ZooKeeper authenticates the client. The client authentication occurs when the client connects to the ZooKeeper service by validating client information.
- Secondly, the authentication framework finds the entries in the ACL, which correspond to the client. ACL entries are pairs that consist of <IDs, Permissions> pairs, where IDs are some strings that identify the client.

An important point about znode ACLs is that the ACL associated with a particular znode doesn't propagate to its children. A client's authentication with ZooKeeper is optional; if the ACLs associated with a znode require a client to authenticate, then it must authenticate using any of the previously mentioned authentication mechanisms. An ACL is the combination of an authentication mechanism, an identity for that mechanism, and a set of permissions.

ZooKeeper's ACLs support the following permissions:

Operation	ACL Permission
CREATE	Creates a child znode
READ	Gets a list of child znodes and the data associated with a znode
WRITE	Sets (writes) data to a znode
DELETE	Deletes a child znode
ADMIN	Sets ACLs (permissions)

Any client that is connecting to a ZooKeeper service has the permission to check the existence of a znode. This `exist` operation is permission-free, which allows to retrieve the stat structure of a znode. We will read about the stat structure of ZooKeeper in the next section.

There are a number of predefined ACLs in ZooKeeper. These IDs, as defined by ZooKeeper ACLs, are shown in the following table:

ACL	Description
ANYONE_ID_UNSAFE	This ID represents anyone
AUTH_IDS	This is used to set ACLs, which get substituted with the IDs of the authenticated client
OPEN_ACL_UNSAFE	This denotes a completely open ACL, and grants all permissions except the ADMIN permission
CREATOR_ALL_ACL	This ACL grants all the permissions to the creator of the znode
READ_ACL_UNSAFE	This ACL gives the world the ability to read

The ZooKeeper stat structure

Every znode in ZooKeeper's namespace has a **stat** structure associated with it, which is analogous to the stat structure of files in a Unix/Linux filesystem. The fields in the stat structure of a znode are shown as follows with their respective meanings:

- cZxid: This is the transaction ID of the change that caused this znode to be created.
- mZxid: This is the transaction ID of the change that last modified this znode.
- pZxid: This is the transaction ID for a znode change that pertains to adding or removing children.

- `ctime`: This denotes the creation time of a znode in milliseconds from epoch.
- `mtime`: This denotes the last modification time of a znode in milliseconds from epoch.
- `dataVersion`: This denotes the number of changes made to the data of this znode.
- `cversion`: This denotes the number of changes made to the children of this znode.
- `aclVersion`: This denotes the number of changes made to the ACL of this znode.
- `ephemeralOwner`: This is the session ID of the znode's owner if the znode is an ephemeral node. If the znode is not an ephemeral node, this field is set to zero.
- `dataLength`: This is the length of the data field of this znode.
- `numChildren`: This denotes the number of children of this znode.

In the ZooKeeper Java shell, the stat structure of a znode can be viewed using the `stat` or `ls2` command. This is illustrated as follows:

- View the znode stat structure using the `stat` command:

```
[zk: localhost(CONNECTED) 0] stat /zookeeper
cZxid = 0x0
ctime = Thu Jan 01 05:30:00 IST 1970
mZxid = 0x0
mtime = Thu Jan 01 05:30:00 IST 1970
pZxid = 0x0
cversion = -1
dataVersion = 0
aclVersion = 0
ephemeralOwner = 0x0
dataLength = 0
numChildren = 1
```

- View the znode stat structure using the `ls2` command:

```
[zk: localhost(CONNECTED) 1] ls2 /zookeeper
[quota]
cZxid = 0x0
ctime = Thu Jan 01 05:30:00 IST 1970
mZxid = 0x0
mtime = Thu Jan 01 05:30:00 IST 1970
pZxid = 0x0
cversion = -1
dataVersion = 0
aclVersion = 0
ephemeralOwner = 0x0
dataLength = 0
numChildren = 1
```

Understanding the inner working of ZooKeeper

So far, we have discussed the basics of the ZooKeeper service and learned in detail about the data model and its attributes. We have also been acquainted with the ZooKeeper watch concept, which is an eventing mechanism that is done when any changes are made to a znode in the ZooKeeper namespace. We read how authentication and a basic security model are implemented by exposing a set of ACLs to be associated with znodes.

In this section, we will discuss and learn about the lifetime of a client's interaction with a ZooKeeper service by introducing the concept of ZooKeeper sessions. We will also read in detail how ZooKeeper works internally by describing its protocols. It is important to know about the inner workings to gain a deep insight, which will help in designing distributed applications with ZooKeeper and understanding the intricacies of the things associated with it.

Let's start with how clients interact with a ZooKeeper service. In order for distributed applications to make use of the ZooKeeper service, they have to use APIs through a client library. ZooKeeper client libraries have language bindings for almost all popular programming languages. The client library is responsible for the interaction of an application with the ZooKeeper service. We will learn about ZooKeeper APIs in the next chapter.

An application's interaction with the ZooKeeper service is illustrated in the following image:

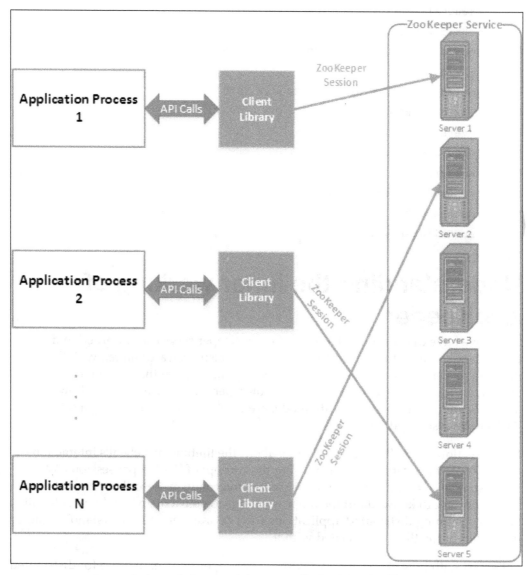

An image that represents how an application interacts with
the ZooKeeper service through client libraries

The ZooKeeper service can run in two modes: standalone and quorum. In the standalone mode, there is a single ZooKeeper server. On the other hand, the quorum mode means that ZooKeeper runs in a replicated mode on a cluster of machines, also known as an **ensemble**.

> The standalone mode is useful only for evaluation and to test application code, but should not be used in production as it's a potential single point of failure. In the quorum mode, ZooKeeper achieves high availability through replication and can provide a service as long as a majority of the machines in the ensemble are up.

The quorum mode

A ZooKeeper quorum constitutes majority of replica nodes that store the most recent state of the ZooKeeper service among all servers in the ensemble. It's basically the minimum number of server nodes that must be up and running and available for client requests. Any update done to the ZooKeeper tree by the clients must be persistently stored in this quorum of nodes for a transaction to be completed successfully.

For example, in a five-node ensemble, any two machines can fail, and we can have a quorum of three servers, and the ZooKeeper service will still work. At a later time, if the other two failed nodes come up, they can sync up the ZooKeeper service state by getting the most recent state from the existing quorum.

> Sizing the number of server nodes in a ZooKeeper service is very important for ZooKeeper to function correctly. As all transaction commits depend upon the concept of majority consensus, it's recommended that a ZooKeeper ensemble should have an odd number of machines in it.

Let's look at an example to see why this makes sense. Suppose we have a ZooKeeper ensemble of five servers. If any two servers fail, the ensemble can still function because a quorum can be formed out of the remaining three nodes. Thus, a five-node ZooKeeper ensemble can tolerate failure of up to two nodes.

Now, for a six-node ensemble, the ZooKeeper service can tolerate a failure of only up to two nodes. This is because with three nodes failing, a quorum can't be formed; a majority consensus can't be achieved there for the ensemble. Again, ZooKeeper quorums must guarantee that any transaction that is acknowledged to the client as a success should be durable and visible across the nodes that form the quorum.

If a ZooKeeper quorum is not formed with the majority nodes in the ensemble, there can be inconsistencies in the state of the ZooKeeper namespace, leading to incorrect results. Apart from node failures, network partitions between the nodes in an ensemble can lead to inconsistent operations as the quorum members won't be able to communicate updates among themselves. This leads to a common problem seen in distributed clusters, called split-brain.

Split-brain is a scenario when two subsets of servers in the ensemble function independently. It leads to an inconsistent state in the whole ZooKeeper service, and different clients get different results for the same request, depending upon the server they are connected to. By having a ZooKeeper cluster running with odd numbers of nodes, we can reduce the chance of such errors to a probabilistic minimum.

Client establishment of sessions with the ZooKeeper service

A client that is connecting to ZooKeeper can be configured with a list of servers that form a ZooKeeper ensemble. A client tries to connect to the servers in the list by picking up a random server from the list. If the connection fails, it tries to connect to the next server, and so on. This process goes on until all the servers in the list have been tried or a successful connection is established.

Once a connection between the client and the ZooKeeper server has been established, a session is created between the client and the server, represented as a 64-bit number, which is assigned to the client. The concept of sessions is very important for the operation of ZooKeeper. A session is associated with every operation a client executes in a ZooKeeper service.

Sessions play a very important role in ZooKeeper. For example, the whole notion of ephemeral znodes is based on the concept of sessions between the client and the ZooKeeper server. Ephemeral znodes have the lifetime of a session being active between a client and ZooKeeper; when this session ends, these nodes are automatically deleted by the ZooKeeper service.

A session has a timeout period, which is specified by the application or the client while connecting to the ZooKeeper service. The client sends a requested timeout as a parameter in the create connection call to create a ZooKeeper, which is specified in milliseconds. If the connection remains idle for more than the timeout period, the session might get expired. Session expiration is managed by the ZooKeeper cluster itself and not by the client. The current implementation requires that the timeout be a minimum of two times the tickTime (see *Chapter 1, A Crash Course in Apache ZooKeeper*) and a maximum of 20 times the tickTime.

Specifying the right session timeout depends on various factors, such as network congestion, complexity of the application logic, and even the size of the ZooKeeper ensemble. For example, in a very busy and congested network, if the latency is high, having a very low session timeout will lead to frequent session expiration. Similarly, it's recommended to have a larger timeout if your ensemble is large. Also, if the application sees frequent connection loss, increasing the session timeout can be useful. However, another caution to that is that it should not have an inadvertent effect on the application's core logic.

Sessions are kept alive by the client sending a **ping request** (heartbeat) to the ZooKeeper service. These heartbeats are sent automatically by the client libraries, and hence, an application programmer need not worry about keeping alive the sessions. Sessions between a client and a ZooKeeper server is maintained using a TCP connection. The interval between two subsequent heartbeats should be kept low, such that connection failure between the client and the ZooKeeper server can be detected quite early and a reconnection attempt can be made. Reconnection to another ZooKeeper server is usually done by the client library in a transparent way. When a reconnection to a different server of the same ensemble is done, the existing sessions and associated ephemeral znodes created by the client remains valid. For single sessions maintained between the client and the server, ZooKeeper guarantees the order, which is typically in the FIFO order.

While reconnect attempts are being made to another ZooKeeper server, the application will receive notifications of disconnections and connections to the service. During this failover, watch notifications are not delivered to the client as the client is typically in a disconnected mode. However, all pending event notifications are dispatched in order when the client successfully reconnects to the service. Also, any client operations are not honored during the reconnection time, and hence, operations will fail. So, it's very important to handle connection-loss scenarios while developing applications with ZooKeeper.

As mentioned in the previous section, an application establishes a session with the ZooKeeper service using a client library. A handle that represents the connection object is returned to the application by the ZooKeeper client API. This ZooKeeper connection object transitions through different states during the period between its creation and its end. The connection object lasts till the connection of the client program is closed gracefully or the session expires because of a timeout.

Once the connection object is created, it starts with the CONNECTING state, and the client library tries to connect to one of the servers in the ZooKeeper ensemble. When connected to the ZooKeeper service, the object transitions to the CONNECTED state. On account of events such as session expiration and authentication failures, or if the application gracefully closes the connection using the library calls, the object's state moves to the CLOSED state.

The state transitions of a ZooKeeper client's session are illustrated in the following image:

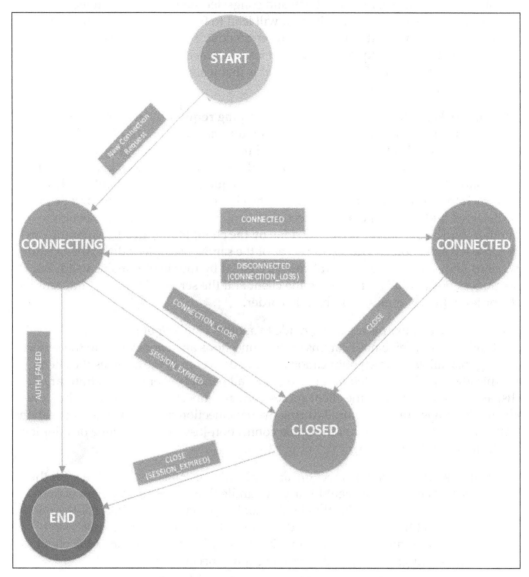

An image that represents the transitions of the ZooKeeper client state

Implementation of ZooKeeper transactions

From the previous sections, we have seen how ZooKeeper runs on an ensemble of servers and how clients connect to these servers, establish a session, and carry out an operation in the ZooKeeper service. Among the ensemble of servers, a server is elected as a leader, and all the remaining servers are made followers. The leader handles all requests that change the ZooKeeper service. Followers receive the updates proposed by the leader, and through a majority consensus mechanism, a consistent state is maintained across the ensemble. The ZooKeeper service takes care of replacing leaders on failures and syncing followers with leaders, and the whole process is fully transparent to client applications.

The service relies on the replication mechanism to ensure that all updates are persistent in all the servers that constitute the ensemble. Each server maintains an in-core database, which represents the entire state of the ZooKeeper namespace. To ensure that updates are durable, and thus recoverable in the event of a server crash, updates are logged to a local disk. Also, the writes are serialized to the disk before they are applied to the in-memory database.

ZooKeeper uses a special atomic messaging protocol called **ZooKeeper Atomic Broadcast (ZAB)**. This protocol ensures that the local replicas in the ensemble never diverge. Also, the ZAB protocol is atomic, so the protocol guarantees that updates either succeed or fail.

The replicated database and the atomic broadcast protocol together with the leader election mechanism form the heart of the ZooKeeper service implementation. An update or a write in the ZooKeeper service namespace, along with a read, is handled by these core components, as you can see in this image (you can also refer to this image at http://zookeeper.apache.org/doc/r3.4.6/zookeeperOver.html#fg_zkComponents):

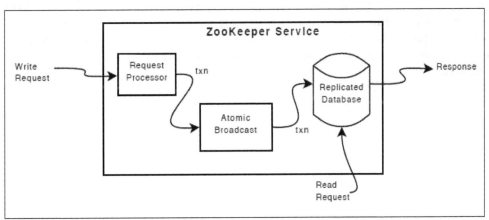

An image that represents the ZooKeeper Service Components

In a ZooKeeper implementation, read requests such as `exists`, `getData`, and `getChildren` are processed locally by the ZooKeeper server where the client is connected. This makes the `read` operations very fast in ZooKeeper. `Write` or `update` requests such as `create`, `delete`, and `setData` are forwarded to the leader in the ensemble. The leader carries out the client request as a transaction. This transaction is similar to the concept of a transaction in a database management system.

A ZooKeeper transaction also comprises all the steps required to successfully execute the request as a single work unit, and the updates are applied atomically. Also, a transaction satisfies the property of isolation, which means that no transaction is interfered with by any other transaction. A transaction in the ZooKeeper service is idempotent. Transactions are identified by a transaction identifier (zxid), which is a 64-bit integer split into two parts: the epoch and the counter, each being 32 bits.

Transaction processing involves two steps in ZooKeeper: leader election and atomic broadcast. This resembles a two-phase commit protocol, which also includes a leader election and an atomic broadcast.

Phase 1 – leader election

The servers in an ensemble go through a process of electing a master server, called the leader. The other servers in the ensemble are called followers.

Each server that participates in the leader election algorithm has a state called `LOOKING`. If a leader already exists in the ensemble, the peer servers inform the new participant servers about the existing leader. After learning about the leader, the new servers sync their state with the leader.

When a leader doesn't exist in the ensemble, ZooKeeper runs a leader election algorithm in the ensemble of servers. In this case, to start with, all of the servers are in the `LOOKING` state. The algorithm dictates the servers to exchange messages to elect a leader. The algorithm stops when the participant servers converge on a common choice for a particular server, which becomes the leader. The server that wins this election enters the `LEADING` state, while the other servers in the ensemble enter the `FOLLOWING` state.

The message exchanged by the participant servers with their peers in the ensemble contains the server's identifier (sid) and the transaction ID (zxid) of the most recent transaction it executed. Each participating server, upon receiving a peer server's message, compares its own sid and zxid with the one it receives. If the received zxid is greater than the one held by the server, the server accepts the received zxid, otherwise, it sets and advertises its own zxid to the peers in the ensemble.

At the end of this algorithm, the server that has the most recent transaction ID (zxid) wins the leader election algorithm. After the algorithm is completed, the follower servers sync their state with the elected leader.

The next step to leader election is leader activation. The newly elected leader proposes a NEW_LEADER proposal, and only after the NEW_LEADER proposal is acknowledged by a majority of servers (quorum) in the ensemble, the leader gets activated. The new leader doesn't accept new proposals until the NEW_LEADER proposal is committed.

Phase 2 – atomic broadcast

All write requests in ZooKeeper are forwarded to the leader. The leader broadcasts the update to the followers in the ensemble. Only after a majority of the followers acknowledge that they have persisted the change does the leader commit the update. ZooKeeper uses the ZAB protocol to achieve consensus, which is designed to be atomic. Thus, an update either succeeds or fails. On a leader failure, the other servers in the ensemble enter a leader election algorithm to elect a new leader among them.

ZAB: High-performance broadcast for primary-backup systems by Junqueira, F.P; Reed, B.C; Serafini. M

(LADIS 2008, in: Proceedings of the 2nd Workshop on Large-Scale Distributed Systems and Middleware)

Readers can access the paper on ZAB from IEEE Xplore in this link: http://bit.ly/1v3N1NN

ZAB guarantees strict ordering in the delivery of transactions as well as in the committing of the transactions. Pictorially, the processing of transactions through atomic messaging can be illustrated as follows:

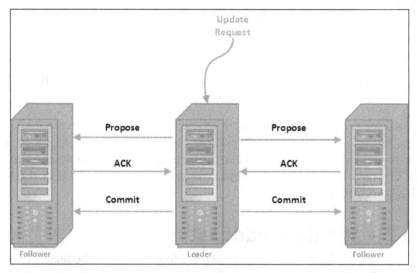

An image that represents the transaction commit protocol of ZooKeeper

The two-phase commit guarantees the ordering of transactions. In the protocol, once the quorum acknowledges a transaction, the leader commits it and a follower records its acknowledgement on disk.

> Apart from leaders and followers, there can be a third personality of a server in a ZooKeeper ensemble, known as observers. Observers and followers are conceptually similar as they both commit proposals from the leader. However, unlike followers, observers do not participate in the voting processes of the two-phase commit process. Observers aid to the scalability of read requests in a ZooKeeper service and help in propagating updates in the ZooKeeper ensemble that span multiple data centers.

Local storage and snapshots

ZooKeeper servers use local storage to persist transactions. The transactions are logged to transaction logs, similar to the approach of sequential append-only log files used in database systems. ZooKeeper servers use pre-allocated files to flush transactions onto disk media. In the two-phase protocol for transaction processing in ZooKeeper, a server acknowledges a proposal only after forcing a write of the transaction to the transaction log. Since ZooKeeper transaction logs are written at great speed, it's very important for the transaction logs to be configured in a disk separate from the boot device of the server.

The servers in the ZooKeeper service also keep on saving point-in-time copies or snapshots of the ZooKeeper tree or the namespace onto the local filesystem. The servers need not coordinate with the other members of the ensemble to save these snapshots. Also, the snapshot processing happens asynchronous to normal functioning of the ZooKeeper server.

The ZooKeeper snapshot files and transactional logs enable recovery of data in times of catastrophic failure or user error. The data directory is specified by the `dataDir` parameter in the ZooKeeper configuration file, and the `data log` directory is specified by the `dataLogDir` parameter.

Summary

In this chapter, we learned the basics of a ZooKeeper service followed by the ZooKeeper data model. We read about the different operations supported by the data model and the eventing mechanism associated with it. We also studied in detail about the intricate details of how ZooKeeper is implemented from the protocol, how it maintains consistency guarantees, transaction-processing through a two-phase atomic broadcast scheme, and so on.

In the next chapter, we will dive into the programming of Apache ZooKeeper. We will learn about the ZooKeeper API model by getting acquainted with the client libraries. In addition to this, we will look at programs to use the APIs, which will be a big stepping stone to writing distributed applications using ZooKeeper.

3
Programming with Apache ZooKeeper

In the previous chapter, we learned about the architecture and internals of ZooKeeper, which gave us an insight into how things work in a ZooKeeper service. So far, from the previous two chapters, we are now well versed with the ZooKeeper data model and the operations supported by it, and we know how to use the ZooKeeper shell (zkCli) to perform the basic ZooKeeper operations. We also read about the API model in ZooKeeper.

In this chapter, we are going to learn how to write client applications with the ZooKeeper client APIs.

Overall, this chapter has been organized into the following topics:

- Programming using the ZooKeeper Java APIs
- Writing ZooKeeper applications with the C library
- Kazoo – a high-level Python library for ZooKeeper

It is assumed that you are familiar with high-level programming languages to follow through the sample code examples. By the end of this chapter, you will feel confident enough to start writing applications using the ZooKeeper APIs.

 The code of this chapter is tested in a Linux operating system, and ZooKeeper version 3.4.6 is used to run the ZooKeeper server instance.

ZooKeeper is developed in Java, and the Java API docs for version 3.4.6 are available at http://zookeeper.apache.org/doc/r3.4.6/api/index.html.

Using the Java client library

The ZooKeeper Java bindings for the development of applications are mainly composed of two Java packages:

- `org.apache.zookeeper`
- `org.apache.zookeeper.data`

The package `org.apache.zookeeper` is composed of the interface definition for ZooKeeper watches and various callback handlers of ZooKeeper. It defines the main class of the ZooKeeper client library along with many static definitions of the ZooKeeper event types and states. The `org.apache.zookeeper.data package` defines the characteristics associated with the data registers, also known as **znodes**, such as **Access Control Lists** (**ACL**), IDs, stats, and so on.

The `org.apache.zookeeper.server`, `org.apache.zookeeper.server.quorum`, and `org.apache.zookeeper.server.upgrade` packages in the ZooKeeper Java APIs are part of the server implementation. The package `org.apache.zookeeper.client` defines the class of *Four Letter Word*, which is used to enquire the state of the ZooKeeper server.

 Refer to *Chapter 1, A Crash Course in Apache ZooKeeper*, for more information on the Four Letter Word class.

Preparing your development environment

Apache ZooKeeper is a complex piece of software, and as such, it requires a lot of other libraries to run. The dependent libraries are shipped with the ZooKeeper distribution as jar files in the `lib` directory. The core ZooKeeper jar file is located in the main tree of the distribution tar ball as `zookeeper-3.4.6.jar`.

To start developing applications for ZooKeeper in Java, we have to set the `CLASSPATH` that points to the ZooKeeper jar and all the allied third-party libraries on which ZooKeeper has dependencies. A script named `zkEnv.sh`, which is shipped with the distribution in the `bin` directory, can be used to set the `CLASSPATH`.

We need to source the script as follows:

```
$ ZOOBINDIR=${ZK_HOME}/bin
$ source ${ZOOBINDIR}/zkEnv.sh
```

The shell variable ZK_HOME is set to the path where ZooKeeper is installed, which, in my setup, is /usr/share/zookeeper. After this, the CLASSPATH variable will be set correctly, which, in my system, looks as follows:

```
$ echo $CLASSPATH
/usr/share/zookeeper-3.4.6/bin/../build/classes
:/usr/share/zookeeper-3.4.6/bin/../build/lib/*.jar
:/usr/share/zookeeper-3.4.6/bin/../lib/slf4j-log4j12-1.6.1.jar
:/usr/share/zookeeper-3.4.6/bin/../lib/slf4j-api-1.6.1.jar
:/usr/share/zookeeper-3.4.6/bin/../lib/netty-3.7.0.Final.jar
:/usr/share/zookeeper-3.4.6/bin/../lib/log4j-1.2.16.jar
:/usr/share/zookeeper-3.4.6/bin/../lib/jline-0.9.94.jar
:/usr/share/zookeeper-3.4.6/bin/../zookeeper-3.4.6.jar
:/usr/share/zookeeper-3.4.6/bin/../src/java/lib/*.jar
:/usr/share/zookeeper-3.4.6/bin/../conf:
```

In the Windows operating system, you will have to run the zkEnv.cmd batch script. The CLASSPATH variable can now be used to compile and run the Java programs written using ZooKeeper APIs. You can source the zkEnv.sh script inside the .bashrc file of your home directory in Unix/Linux in order to avoid sourcing it every time you start a shell session.

The first ZooKeeper program

To get introduced with the ZooKeeper Java API, let's start with a very simple program that does the job of connecting to a ZooKeeper instance in the localhost, and if the connection is successful, it prints the list of znodes in the root path '/' of the ZooKeeper namespace.

The code for this program is shown as follows:

```java
/*Our First ZooKeeper Program*/
import java.io.IOException;
import java.util.ArrayList;
import java.util.List;
import org.apache.zookeeper.KeeperException;
import org.apache.zookeeper.ZooKeeper;
public class HelloZooKeeper {
  public static void main(String[] args) throws IOException {
    String hostPort = "localhost:2181";
    String zpath = "/";
    List <String> zooChildren = new ArrayList<String>();
    ZooKeeper zk = new ZooKeeper(hostPort, 2000, null);
    if (zk != null) {
      try {
        zooChildren = zk.getChildren(zpath, false);
```

```
        System.out.println("Znodes of '/': ");
        for (String child: zooChildren) {
          //print the children
          System.out.println(child);
        }
      } catch (KeeperException e) {
        e.printStackTrace();
      } catch (InterruptedException e) {
        e.printStackTrace();
      }
    }
  }
}
```

Before we build and execute the preceding code fragment, let's look into the details of what it actually does. The code begins with the `import` statements. Using these statements, we imported the packages required by the various components of the program. As mentioned previously, the `org.apache.zookeeper` package contains all the required classes and interfaces for a client to interact with the ZooKeeper server. After importing the packages, we defined a class called `HelloZooKeeper` with a `main` function. As we are going to connect to the ZooKeeper instance that is running in the same system, we define the host and port string as `localhost:2181` in the `main` function. The code line `zk = new ZooKeeper(hostPort, 2000, null)` calls the ZooKeeper constructor, which tries to connect to the ZooKeeper server and returns a handle to it. In the previous chapter, we learned that for a client program to connect to a ZooKeeper server instance and maintain that connection, it needs to maintain a live session. The handle returned by the constructor, `zk` in our case, represents this session. The ZooKeeper API is built around this handle, and every method call requires a handle to execute.

The constructor of the `ZooKeeper` class creates a handle to the ZooKeeper instance with the following code:

```
ZooKeeper(String connectString, int sessionTimeout,
Watcher watcher)
```

The parameters used are explained as follows:

*   `connectString`: This is a comma-separated list of host:port pairs, each of which corresponds to a ZooKeeper server. For example, `10.0.0.1:2001`, `10.0.0.2:2002`, and `10.0.0.3:2003` represent a valid host:port pair for a ZooKeeper ensemble of three nodes.

*   `sessionTimeout`: This is the session timeout in milliseconds. This is the amount of time ZooKeeper waits without getting a heartbeat from the client before declaring the session as dead.

- watcher: A watcher object, which, if created, will be notified of state changes and node events. This watcher object needs to be created separately through a user-defined class by implementing the Watcher interface and passing the instantiated object to the ZooKeeper constructor. A client application can get a notification for various types of events such as connection loss, session expiry, and so on. We will look at implementing a Watcher interface in the next section of this chapter.

The ZooKeeper Java API defines three more constructors with additional argument parameters, to specify more advanced operations. These are shown in the following code:

```
ZooKeeper(String connectString, int sessionTimeout,
Watcher watcher, boolean canBeReadOnly)
```

In the preceding constructor of the ZooKeeper class, the additional boolean canBeReadOnly parameter, if set to true, allows the created client to go to the read-only mode in case of network partitioning. The read-only mode is a scenario in which a client can't find any majority servers but there's a partitioned server that it can reach; it connects to it in a read-only mode such that read requests to the server are allowed but write requests are not. The client continues to attempt to connect to majority servers in the background, while still maintaining the read-only mode. Partitioned servers are merely a subset of the ZooKeeper ensemble, which is formed due to network portioning in the cluster. Majority servers constitute the majority quorum in the ensemble.

The following constructor shows two additional parameters:

```
ZooKeeper(String connectString, int sessionTimeout, Watcher watcher,
long sessionId, byte[] sessionPasswd)
```

This constructor allows a ZooKeeper client object to be created with two additional parameters:

- sessionId: In case the client is reconnecting to the ZooKeeper server, a specific session ID can be used to refer to the previously connected session
- sessionPasswd: If the specified session requires a password, this can be specified here

The following constructor is a combination of the previous two calls:

```
ZooKeeper(String connectString, int sessionTimeout,
Watcher watcher, long sessionId, byte[] sessionPasswd,
boolean canBeReadOnly)
```

This constructor is a combination of the previous two calls, which allows reconnecting to a specified session with the read-only mode enabled.

 The detailed Java API doc of the ZooKeeper class can be read at http://zookeeper.apache.org/doc/r3.4.6/api/index.html.

Now, let's go back to our ZooKeeper program. After calling the constructor, we will get a handle to the ZooKeeper server if our connection is successful. We pass the handle to a getChildren method with the following code:

```
zooChildren = zk.getChildren(zpath, false)
```

The getChildren (String path, boolean watch) method of the ZooKeeper class returns a list of the children of a znode at a given path. We simply iterate the list returned by this method and print the child string to the console.

We name our program HelloZooKeeper.java, and compile our program as follows:

```
$ javac -cp $CLASSPATH HelloZooKeeper.java
```

Before we run our program, we need to start our ZooKeeper server instance, if it's not already started, with the following command:

```
$ ${ZK_HOME}/bin/zkServer.sh start
```

Let's run our program as follows:

```
$ java -cp $CLASSPATH HelloZooKeeper
```

Executing the programs prints a lot of log messages in the console screen, showing us the version of ZooKeeper used, the Java version, Java class paths, the architecture of the server, and so on. A snippet of these log messages is shown here:

```
$ java -cp $CLASSPATH HelloZooKeeper
- INFO  - Client environment:zookeeper.version=3.4.6-1569965, built on 02/20/2014 09:09 GMT
- INFO  - Client environment:host.name=ubuntu
- INFO  - Client environment:java.version=1.7.0_67
- INFO  - Client environment:java.vendor=Oracle Corporation
- INFO  - Client environment:java.home=/usr/java/jdk1.7.0_67/jre
- INFO  - Initiating client connection, connectString=localhost:2181 sessionTimeout=2000 watcher=null
- INFO  - Socket connection established to localhost/127.0.0.1:2181, initiating session
- INFO - Session establishment complete on server localhost/127.0.0.1:2181,
sessionid = 0x1498d63efe30002, negotiated timeout = 4000
```

The log messages generated by the ZooKeeper Java APIs are very useful for debugging purposes. It gives us invaluable information about what's really going on behind the scenes when a client connects to the ZooKeeper server, establishes a session, and so on. The last three log messages shown previously tell us how the client is initiating a connection with the parameters specified in our program and how, after a successful connection, the server doles out a session ID to the client.

Finally, a successful execution of our program prints out the following in the console:

```
Znodes of '/':
zookeeper
```

We can verify the correctness of our program using the ZooKeeper shell:

```
$ $ZK_HOME/bin/zkCli.sh -server localhost
```

```
[zk: localhost(CONNECTED) 0] ls /
[zookeeper]
```

Congratulations! We have just successfully written our first ZooKeeper client program.

Implementing a Watcher interface

We have read in detail about the ZooKeeper watches in the previous chapter. Watches enable a client to receive notifications from the ZooKeeper server and process these events upon occurrence. ZooKeeper Java APIs provide a public interface called Watcher, which a client event handler class must implement in order to receive notifications about events from the ZooKeeper server it connects to. Programmatically, an application that uses such a client handles these events by registering a callback object with the client.

In this section, we will read about implementing a watcher, which handles events generated by ZooKeeper when the data associated with a znode changes.

The Watcher interface is declared in the org.apache.zookeeper package as follows:

```
public interface Watcher {
  void process(WatchedEvent event);
}
```

To illustrate the znode data watcher, we will have two Java classes: DataWatcher
and DataUpdater. DataWatcher will run continuously and listen for the
NodeDataChange events from the ZooKeeper server in a specific znode path called
/MyConfig. The DataUpdater class will periodically update the data field in this
znode path, which will generate events, and upon receiving these events, the
DataWatcher class will print the changed data onto the console.

The following is the code of the DataWatcher.java class:

```java
import java.io.IOException;
import org.apache.zookeeper.CreateMode;
import org.apache.zookeeper.KeeperException;
import org.apache.zookeeper.WatchedEvent;
import org.apache.zookeeper.Watcher;
import org.apache.zookeeper.ZooDefs;
import org.apache.zookeeper.ZooKeeper;
public class DataWatcher implements Watcher, Runnable {
  private static String hostPort = "localhost:2181";
  private static String zooDataPath = "/MyConfig";
  byte zoo_data[] = null;
  ZooKeeper zk;
  public DataWatcher() {
    try {
      zk = new ZooKeeper(hostPort, 2000, this);
      if (zk != null) {
        try {
```

Create the znode if it doesn't exist, with the following code:

```java
        if (zk.exists(zooDataPath, this) == null) {
          zk.create(zooDataPath, "".getBytes(),
          ZooDefs.Ids.OPEN_ACL_UNSAFE,
          CreateMode.PERSISTENT);
        }
      } catch (KeeperException | InterruptedException e) {
        e.printStackTrace();
      }
    }
  } catch (IOException e) {
```

```
      e.printStackTrace();
    }
  }
  public void printData()
  throws InterruptedException, KeeperException {
    zoo_data = zk.getData(zooDataPath, this, null);
    String zString = new String(zoo_data);
```

The following code prints the current content of the znode to the console:

```
    System.out.printf("\nCurrent Data @ ZK Path %s: %s",
    zooDataPath, zString);
  }
  @Override
  public void process(WatchedEvent event) {
    System.out.printf(
    "\nEvent Received: %s", event.toString());
    //We will process only events of type NodeDataChanged
    if (event.getType() == Event.EventType.NodeDataChanged) {
      try {
        printData();
      } catch (InterruptedException e) {
        e.printStackTrace();
      } catch (KeeperException e) {
        e.printStackTrace();
      }
    }
  }
  public static void main(String[] args)
  throws InterruptedException, KeeperException {
    DataWatcher dataWatcher = new DataWatcher();
    dataWatcher.printData();
    dataWatcher.run();
  }
  public void run() {
    try {
      synchronized (this) {
        while (true) {
          wait();
        }
      }
    } catch (InterruptedException e) {
      e.printStackTrace();
      Thread.currentThread().interrupt();
    }
  }
}
```

Let's do a code walkthrough of the DataWatcher.java class to understand the implementation of a ZooKeeper watcher. The DataWatcher public class implements the Watcher interface along with the Runnable interface, as we plan to run the watcher as a thread. The main method creates an instance of the DataWatcher class. In the preceding code, the DataWatcher constructor tries to connect to the ZooKeeper instance that is running on localhost. If the connection is successful, we check whether the znode path /MyConfig exists, with the following code:

```
if (zk.exists(zooDataPath, this) == null) {
```

If the znode is not present in the ZooKeeper namespace, the exists method call returns NULL, and we try to create it as a persistent znode with the code as follows:

```
zk.create(zooDataPath, "".getBytes(),
    ZooDefs.Ids.OPEN_ACL_UNSAFE,
    CreateMode.PERSISTENT);
```

Next is the process method, which is declared in the Watcher interface of org.apache.ZooKeeper, and implemented here by the DataWatcher class, by using the following code:

```
public void process(WatchedEvent event) {
```

To keep things simple, in the process method, we print the event received from the ZooKeeper instance and do further processing only for the event of type NodeDataChanged as follows:

```
if (event.getType() == Event.EventType.NodeDataChanged)
```

When an event of type NodeDataChanged is received due to any update or change in the data field of the znode path /MyConfig, we call the printData method to print the current content of the znode. Observe carefully here that when we perform a getData call on the znode, we set a watch again, which is the second parameter of the method, as shown in the following code:

```
zoo_data = zk.getData(zooDataPath, this, null);
```

From the previous chapter, recall that a watch event is a one-time trigger that is sent to the client that sets the watch, and to keep receiving further event notifications, the client should reset the watch.

The DataUpdater (DataUpdater.java) is a simple class, which connects to the ZooKeeper instance that runs the localhost and updates the data field of the znode path /MyConfig with a random string. Here, we chose to update the znode with a **Universally Unique IDentifier (UUID)** string since a subsequent call of the UUID generator is guaranteed to generate a unique string.

The `DataUpdater.java` class can be constructed as follows:

```java
import java.io.IOException;
import java.util.UUID;
import org.apache.zookeeper.KeeperException;
import org.apache.zookeeper.WatchedEvent;
import org.apache.zookeeper.Watcher;
import org.apache.zookeeper.ZooKeeper;
public class DataUpdater implements Watcher {
  private static String hostPort = "localhost:2181";
  private static String zooDataPath = "/MyConfig";
  ZooKeeper zk;
  public DataUpdater() throws IOException {
    try {
      zk = new ZooKeeper(hostPort, 2000, this);
    } catch (IOException e) {
      e.printStackTrace();
    }
  }
}
```

The `DataUpdater` class updates the znode path `/MyConfig` every 5 seconds with a new UUID string. This is shown in the following code:

```java
public void run() throws InterruptedException, KeeperException {
  while (true) {
    String uuid = UUID.randomUUID().toString();
    byte zoo_data[] = uuid.getBytes();
    zk.setData(zooDataPath, zoo_data, -1);
    try {
      Thread.sleep(5000); // Sleep for 5 secs
    } catch(InterruptedException e) {
      Thread.currentThread().interrupt();
    }
  }
}
```

The preceding code makes the ZooKeeper server trigger a `NodeDataChanged` event. Since `DataWatcher` had set a watch for this znode path, it receives the notification for the data change event. It then retrieves the updated data, resets the watch, and prints the data on the console.

Finally, the main method is created as follows:

```
public static void main(String[] args) throws
IOException, InterruptedException, KeeperException {
  DataUpdater dataUpdater = new DataUpdater();
  dataUpdater.run();
}
@Override
public void process(WatchedEvent event) {
  System.out.printf("\nEvent Received: %s", event.toString());
}
}
```

Let's compile both our `DataWatcher` and `DataUpdater` classes using the following commands:

$ javac -cp $CLASSPATH DataWatcher.java

$ javac -cp $CLASSPATH DataUpdater.java

To execute the watcher and updater, open two terminal windows. We need to run the watcher first as it creates the znode named `/MyConfig` if not already created in the ZooKeeper's namespace. Make sure that the ZooKeeper server is running in the `localhost` before you run the watcher.

In one of the terminal windows, we execute the watcher class by running the following command:

$ java -cp $CLASSPATH DataWatcher

This outputs a message similar to the one shown in the following screenshot:

```
$ java -cp $CLASSPATH DataWatcher
- INFO - Initiating client connection, connectString=localhost:2181 sessionTimeout=2000
watcher=DataWatcher@4993d44d
- INFO - Session establishment complete on server localhost/127.0.0.1:2181,
sessionid = 0x1498d63efe30004, negotiated timeout = 4000

Event Received: WatchedEvent state:SyncConnected type:None path:null
Event Received: WatchedEvent state:SyncConnected type:NodeCreated path:/MyConfig
Current Data @ ZK Path /MyConfig: █
```

As shown in the preceding screenshot, the znode path `/MyConfig` is created by the `DataWatcher` class. It also prints the content of the znode, but nothing gets printed in the console as we did not set any data while creating the znode. When the znode gets created, the watcher in our class received an event notification of the type `NodeCreated`, which gets printed in the console. The `DataWatcher` class continues to run and listen for events `/MyConfig` from the ZooKeeper server.

Let's run the `DataUpdater` class in another terminal window:

```
$ java -cp $CLASSPATH DataUpdater
```

The `DataUpdater` class continues to run silently after logging the initial ZooKeeper-specific log messages into the console. It sets a new UUID string into the data field of the ZooKeeper path /MyConfig. As a result of this, we will see that every 5 seconds, something similar to the output shown in the following screenshot gets printed in the terminal window where `DataWatcher` is running:

```
Current Data @ ZK Path /MyConfig:
Event Received: WatchedEvent state:SyncConnected type:NodeDataChanged path:/MyConfig
Current Data @ ZK Path /MyConfig: f31e2892-ad84-4243-99a6-f41dcaa63725
Event Received: WatchedEvent state:SyncConnected type:NodeDataChanged path:/MyConfig
Current Data @ ZK Path /MyConfig: 6c619ce0-3d0a-48e2-8059-835178de8695
Event Received: WatchedEvent state:SyncConnected type:NodeDataChanged path:/MyConfig
Current Data @ ZK Path /MyConfig: f43110df-a37f-4904-8472-1f3a1f1607ac
Event Received: WatchedEvent state:SyncConnected type:NodeDataChanged path:/MyConfig
Current Data @ ZK Path /MyConfig: a56da15e-1afd-4cfe-97a0-2addaa67a588
Event Received: WatchedEvent state:SyncConnected type:NodeDataChanged path:/MyConfig
Current Data @ ZK Path /MyConfig: 0792bbf7-b2d3-4b18-931e-fc9851f011f1
Event Received: WatchedEvent state:SyncConnected type:NodeDataChanged path:/MyConfig
Current Data @ ZK Path /MyConfig: 5fcd87c0-e11a-44db-8878-b11e9e3fd899
Event Received: WatchedEvent state:SyncConnected type:NodeDataChanged path:/MyConfig
Current Data @ ZK Path /MyConfig: ef103c0e-88b9-4b51-a33d-e7737ac74b23
```

The `DataWatcher` can also be tested using the ZooKeeper shell. Keep running the `DataWatcher` class in a terminal as before, and in another terminal, invoke the ZooKeeper shell and run the command shown in the following screenshot:

```
[zk: localhost(CONNECTED) 0] set /MyConfig "HelloZooKeeper"
cZxid = 0x205
ctime = Sat Nov 08 09:15:52 IST 2014
mZxid = 0x212
mtime = Sat Nov 08 09:33:56 IST 2014
pZxid = 0x205
cversion = 0
dataVersion = 8
aclVersion = 0
ephemeralOwner = 0x0
dataLength = 16
numChildren = 0
[zk: localhost(CONNECTED) 1]
```

In the terminal where the `DataWatcher` is running, the following message gets printed:

```
Event Received: WatchedEvent state:SyncConnected type:NodeDataChanged path:/MyConfig
Current Data @ ZK Path /MyConfig: "HelloZooKeeper"
```

Example – a cluster monitor

Popular services offered over the Internet, such as e-mail, file-serving platforms, online gaming, and so on, are served through highly available clusters of hundreds or thousands of servers spanned over multiple data centers, which are often geographically apart. In such clusters, a few dedicated server nodes are set up to monitor the aliveness of the servers, which hosts the services or applications in the production network. In a cloud computing environment, such monitoring nodes, which are also used to administer the cloud environment, are referred to as cloud controllers. An important job for these controller nodes is to detect the failure of the production servers in real time, and accordingly notify the administrator and also take necessary actions, such as failing over the applications from the failed server to another server, thereby ensuring fault tolerance and high availability.

In this section, we'll develop a minimalistic distributed cluster monitor model using the ZooKeeper Java client APIs. Building this monitoring model using the ephemeral znode concept of ZooKeeper is fairly simple and elegant, as described in the following steps:

1. Every production server runs a ZooKeeper client as a daemon process. This process connects to the ZooKeeper server and creates an ephemeral znode with a name, preferably its network name or host name under a predefined path in the ZooKeeper namespace, say `/Members`.

2. The cloud controller node(s) runs a ZooKeeper watcher process, which keeps a watch on the path `/Members` and listens for events of the type `NodeChildrenChanged`. This watcher process runs as a service or daemon and sets/resets watches on the path, and has the logic implemented to call the appropriate module to take necessary actions for watch events.

3. Now, if a production server goes down due to hardware failure or software crash, the ZooKeeper client process gets killed, causing the session between the server and the ZooKeeper service to get terminated. Owing to the unique property of ephemeral znodes, whenever the client connection goes down, the ZooKeeper service automatically deletes the znode in the path `/Members`.

4. The deletion of the znode in the path raises a `NodeChildrenChanged` event, and as a result, the watcher process in the cloud controller gets a notification. By calling a `getChildren` method in the path `/Members`, it can figure out which server node has gone down.

5. The controller node can then take the appropriate actions, such as spawning off the recovery logic to restart the faulted services in another server.

6. This logic can be built to work in real time, guaranteeing for near-zero downtime and highly available services.

To implement this cluster-monitoring model, we will develop two Java classes. The class ClusterMonitor will continuously run a watcher to keep a watch on the path /Members in the ZooKeeper tree. After processing the raised events, we will print the list of znodes in the console and reset the watch. The other class ClusterClient will initiate a connection to the ZooKeeper server, creating an ephemeral znode under /Members.

To emulate a cluster with multiple nodes, we will start many clients on the same machine and create the ephemeral znodes with the process IDs of the client processes. By looking at the process ID, the ClusterMonitor class can figure out which client process has gone down and which ones are still alive. In a real-life scenario, the client processes will usually create ephemeral znodes with the hostname of the server that they are currently running on. The source codes of the two classes are shown next.

The ClusterMonitor.java class can be constructed as follows:

```java
import java.io.IOException;
import java.util.List;
import org.apache.zookeeper.CreateMode;
import org.apache.zookeeper.KeeperException;
import org.apache.zookeeper.WatchedEvent;
import org.apache.zookeeper.Watcher;
import org.apache.zookeeper.ZooDefs.Ids;
import org.apache.zookeeper.ZooKeeper;
public class ClusterMonitor implements Runnable {
private static String membershipRoot = "/Members";
private final Watcher connectionWatcher;
private final Watcher childrenWatcher;
private ZooKeeper zk;
boolean alive=true;
public ClusterMonitor(String HostPort) throws
   IOException, InterruptedException, KeeperException {
    connectionWatcher = new Watcher() {
      @Override
      public void process(WatchedEvent event) {
        if(event.getType()==Watcher.Event.EventType.None &&
          event.getState() ==
          Watcher.Event.KeeperState.SyncConnected) {
            System.out.printf("\nEvent Received: %s",
              event.toString());
        }
      }
    };

    childrenWatcher = new Watcher() {
```

```
      @Override
      public void process(WatchedEvent event) {
        System.out.printf("\nEvent Received: %s",
          event.toString());
        if (event.getType() ==
          Event.EventType.NodeChildrenChanged) {
            try {
              //Get current list of child znode,
              //reset the watch
              List<String> children = zk.getChildren(
                membershipRoot, this);
              wall("!!!Cluster Membership Change!!!");
              wall("Members: " + children);
            } catch (KeeperException e) {
              throw new RuntimeException(e);
            } catch (InterruptedException e) {
              Thread.currentThread().interrupt();
              alive = false;
              throw new RuntimeException(e);
            }
        }
      }
    };

    zk = new ZooKeeper(HostPort, 2000, connectionWatcher);

    // Ensure the parent znode exists
    if(zk.exists(membershipRoot, false) == null) {
      zk.create(membershipRoot, "ClusterMonitorRoot".getBytes(),
        Ids.OPEN_ACL_UNSAFE, CreateMode.PERSISTENT);
    }

    // Set a watch on the parent znode
    List<String> children = zk.getChildren(membershipRoot,
      childrenWatcher);
    System.err.println("Members: " + children);
  }

  public synchronized void close() {
    try {
      zk.close();
    } catch (InterruptedException e) {
      e.printStackTrace();
    }
  }
}
```

```
    public void wall (String message) {
      System.out.printf("\nMESSAGE: %s", message);
    }

    public void run() {
      try {
        synchronized (this) {
          while (alive) {
            wait();
          }
        }
      } catch (InterruptedException e) {
        e.printStackTrace();
        Thread.currentThread().interrupt();
      } finally {
        this.close();
      }
    }

    public static void main(String[] args) throws
      IOException, InterruptedException, KeeperException {
      if (args.length != 1) {
        System.err.println("Usage: ClusterMonitor <Host:Port>");
        System.exit(0);
      }
      String hostPort = args[0];
      new ClusterMonitor(hostPort).run();
    }
}
```

The ClusterClient.java class can be constructed as follows:

```
import java.io.IOException;
import java.lang.management.ManagementFactory;
import org.apache.zookeeper.CreateMode;
import org.apache.zookeeper.KeeperException;
import org.apache.zookeeper.WatchedEvent;
import org.apache.zookeeper.Watcher;
import org.apache.zookeeper.ZooDefs.Ids;
import org.apache.zookeeper.ZooKeeper;
public class ClusterClient implements Watcher, Runnable {
private static String membershipRoot = "/Members";
ZooKeeper zk;
public ClusterClient(String hostPort, Long pid) {
```

```java
String processId = pid.toString();
try {
  zk = new ZooKeeper(hostPort, 2000, this);
} catch (IOException e) {
  e.printStackTrace();
}
if (zk != null) {
  try {
    zk.create(membershipRoot + '/' + processId,
      processId.getBytes(),
      Ids.OPEN_ACL_UNSAFE, CreateMode.EPHEMERAL);
  } catch (
    KeeperException | InterruptedException e) {
      e.printStackTrace();
    }
  }
}

public synchronized void close() {
  try {
    zk.close();
  }
  catch (InterruptedException e) {
    e.printStackTrace();
      }
}

@Override
public void process(WatchedEvent event) {
  System.out.printf("\nEvent Received: %s", event.toString());
}

public void run() {
  try {
    synchronized (this) {
      while (true) {
        wait();
        }
    }
  } catch (InterruptedException e) {
    e.printStackTrace();
    Thread.currentThread().interrupt();
  } finally {
    this.close();
```

```
      }
   }

   public static void main(String[] args) {
      if (args.length != 1) {
         System.err.println("Usage: ClusterClient <Host:Port>");
         System.exit(0);
      }
      String hostPort = args[0];
      //Get the process id
      String name = ManagementFactory.getRuntimeMXBean().getName();
      int index = name.indexOf('@');
      Long processId = Long.parseLong(name.substring(0, index));
      new ClusterClient(hostPort, processId).run();
   }
}
```

Let's compile both these classes as follows:

```
$ javac -cp $CLASSPATH ClusterMonitor.java
$ javac -cp $CLASSPATH ClusterClient.java
```

To execute the cluster-monitoring model, open two terminals. In one of the terminals, we will run the ClusterMonitor class. In another terminal, we will execute more than one instance of the ClusterClient class by running it in the background.

In the first terminal, execute the ClusterMonitor class as follows:

```
$ java -cp $CLASSPATH ClusterMonitorlocalhost:2181
```

As shown in the previous examples, we will see debug log messages from the client APIs, and finally, the ClusterMonitor class will start watching for events with the output as follows:

```
$ java -cp $CLASSPATH ClusterMonitor
Usage: ClusterMonitor <Host:Port>
$ java -cp $CLASSPATH ClusterMonitor localhost:2181

- INFO - Session establishment complete on server localhost/127.0.0.1:2181,
sessionid = 0x1498d63efe30008, negotiated timeout = 4000


Event Received: WatchedEvent state:SyncConnected type:None path:nullMembers: []
```

Now, let's execute five instances of the ClusterClient class to simulate five nodes of a cluster. The ClusterClient creates ephemeral znodes with its own process ID in the /Members path of the ZooKeeper tree:

```
$ java -cp $CLASSPATH ClusterClient localhost:2181 2>&1>/dev/null &
[1] 4028
$ java -cp $CLASSPATH ClusterClient localhost:2181 2>&1>/dev/null &
[2] 4045
$ java -cp $CLASSPATH ClusterClient localhost:2181 2>&1>/dev/null &
[3] 4057
$ java -cp $CLASSPATH ClusterClient localhost:2181 2>&1>/dev/null &
[4] 4072
$ java -cp $CLASSPATH ClusterClient localhost:2181 2>&1>/dev/null &
[5] 4084
```

Corresponding to this, we will observe that our ClusterMonitor class detects these new ClusterClient class instances coming up, as it was watching for events in the /Members path of the ZooKeeper tree. This emulates a Node Join event in a real cluster. You can see the output in the terminal where the ClusterMonitor class is running, and this is similar to the one shown in the following screenshot:

```
Event Received: WatchedEvent state:SyncConnected type:NodeChildrenChanged path:/Members
MESSAGE: !!! Cluster Membership Change !!!
MESSAGE: Members: [3987]
Event Received: WatchedEvent state:SyncConnected type:NodeChildrenChanged path:/Members
MESSAGE: !!! Cluster Membership Change !!!
MESSAGE: Members: []
Event Received: WatchedEvent state:SyncConnected type:NodeChildrenChanged path:/Members
MESSAGE: !!! Cluster Membership Change !!!
MESSAGE: Members: [4028]
Event Received: WatchedEvent state:SyncConnected type:NodeChildrenChanged path:/Members
MESSAGE: !!! Cluster Membership Change !!!
MESSAGE: Members: [4028, 4045]
Event Received: WatchedEvent state:SyncConnected type:NodeChildrenChanged path:/Members
MESSAGE: !!! Cluster Membership Change !!!
MESSAGE: Members: [4028, 4057, 4045]
Event Received: WatchedEvent state:SyncConnected type:NodeChildrenChanged path:/Members
MESSAGE: !!! Cluster Membership Change !!!
MESSAGE: Members: [4072, 4028, 4057, 4045]
Event Received: WatchedEvent state:SyncConnected type:NodeChildrenChanged path:/Members
MESSAGE: !!! Cluster Membership Change !!!
MESSAGE: Members: [4072, 4028, 4084, 4057, 4045]
```

Now, if we kill a `ClusterClient java` process, the session that it was maintaining with the ZooKeeper server will get terminated. As a result of this, the ephemeral znode that the client had created will be deleted. The deletion will trigger a `NodeChildrenChanged` event, which will be caught by the `ClusterMonitor` class. This emulates a `Node Leave` scenario in a cluster.

Let's terminate the `ClusterClient` process with the ID `4084`:

```
$ kill -9 4084
```

The following screenshot shows the output in the terminal of the `ClusterMonitor` class. It lists the currently available processes with their process IDs, which emulates live servers:

```
Event Received: WatchedEvent state:SyncConnected type:NodeChildrenChanged path:/Members
MESSAGE: !!! Cluster Membership Change !!!
MESSAGE: Members: [4072, 4028, 4057, 4045]
```

The preceding example implementation of a simple yet elegant cluster-monitoring model shows the real power of ZooKeeper. In the absence of ZooKeeper, developing such a model that monitors the aliveness of nodes in real time will be a real Herculean task.

The C client library

ZooKeeper is shipped with an official C client library, which can be used to develop distributed applications in C/C++. Many of the other language bindings such as the Python client binding shipped with ZooKeeper distribution are built using the C library. In this section, we will learn about the C client APIs and illustrate their usage by developing a znode data-watcher client.

In the *Connecting to ZooKeeper with C-based shell* section of *Chapter 1, A Crash Course in Apache ZooKeeper*, we learned how to build the ZooKeeper C library and the C-based shell using the `make` command. Once we build the C library, the following two shared libraries get built:

- The multi-threaded library:`libzookeeper_mt.so.2.0.0`
- The single-thread library:`libzookeeper_st.so.2.0.0`

The libraries are usually installed in `/usr/local/lib`. You need to have this path exported through your `LD_LIBRARY_PATH` environment variables for the applications to find the libraries.

The multi-threaded library is most commonly used and recommended. It provides both the synchronous as well as the asynchronous APIs. This library functions by creating an I/O thread and an event dispatch thread to handle connections and event callbacks. The single-thread library provides only the asynchronous APIs and callbacks. This library is used only on platforms where the *pthread* library is not available.

The C header file `zookeeper.h` in `src/c/include` in the ZooKeeper distribution outlines the main reference for the C client APIs. The ZooKeeper C command line shell's implementation is available in `src/c/src` as `cli.c`. Readers are advised to go through this code to understand how client applications are written using the ZooKeeper C API.

Getting started with the C API

The ZooKeeper C API provides a way for the client to create a session with the ZooKeeper server through a handle. The handle represents a connection to the ZooKeeper service and is needed to invoke any ZooKeeper function. A handle is declared as type `zhandle_t`, and is obtained by calling the `zookeeper_init` function:

```
ZOOAPI zhandle_t*
zookeeper_init (
   const char *host,        /* comma separated host:port pairs */
   watcher_fn  fn,          /* watcher callback function */
   int recv_timeout,        /* session expiration time */
   const clientid_t *clientid, /* session id for reconnection */
   void *context,    /* context of the handle object */
   int  flags        /* for future use, should be set to zero*/
)
```

The `zookeeper_init` function returns a handle, which is a pointer to the opaque `zhandle` structure and is used to communicate with the ZooKeeper service. Also, a `zookeeper` session gets established after this call, which corresponds to the handle. If the function fails to create a new `zhandle` structure, it returns NULL, and the error is set accordingly. The session establishment is asynchronous and hence the session should not be considered established until (and unless) an event of the state ZOO_CONNECTED_STATE is received by the client program. This event can be processed by implementing a watcher function with the following signature:

```
typedef void
(* watcher_fn)(
   zhandle_t *zh, /* the zookeeper handle */
   int type,/* event type, e.g. ZOO_SESSION_EVENT */
```

```
    int state,/* connection state, e.g. ZOO_CONNECTED_STATE */
    const char *path, /* znode path for which the watcher is
    triggered. NULL for session events */
    void *watcherCtx/* watcher context object */
)
```

Having seen how to connect to a ZooKeeper service, let's now write a simple program to connect to the ZooKeeper service and list the children under the / root znode path.

The source code for our ZooKeeper client that uses the C library follows next.

Let's name this file `hello_zookeeper.c`:

```c
#include <stdio.h>
#include "zookeeper.h"
static zhandle_t *zh;
typedef struct String_vector zoo_string;
/* An empty Watcher function */
void my_watcher_func(zhandle_t *zzh, int type, int state,
const char *path, void *watcherCtx) {}
/* Main Function */
int
main(int argc, char *argv[])
{
  int i, retval;
  char *host_port = "localhost:2181";
  char *zoo_root = "/";
  zoo_string *children_list =
    (zoo_string *) malloc(sizeof(zoo_string));
  /* Connect to ZooKeeper server */
  zh = zookeeper_init(host_port, my_watcher_func,
    2000, 0, NULL, 0);
  if (zh == NULL)
  {
    fprintf(stderr, "Error connecting  to ZooKeeper server!\n");
    exit(EXIT_FAILURE);
  }
  /* Get the list of children synchronously */
  retval = zoo_get_children(zh, zoo_root, 0, children_list);
  if (retval != ZOK)
  {
    fprintf(stderr, "Error retrieving znode from path %s!\n",
      zoo_root);
    exit(EXIT_FAILURE);
  }
```

```
fprintf(stderr, "\n=== znode listing === [ %s ]", zoo_root);
for (i = 0; i < children_list->count; i++)
{
   fprintf(stderr, "\n(%d): %s", i+1, children_list->data[i]);
}
fprintf(stderr, "\n=== done ===\n");
/* Finally close the ZooKeeper handle */
zookeeper_close(zh);
return 0;
}
```

Assuming the ZooKeeper C client-shared libraries are installed in /usr/local/lib, we can compile the preceding program as follows:

```
$ gcc -Wall hello_zookeeper.c -o hello_zookeeper
-I${ZK_HOME}/src/c/include -I${ZK_HOME}/src/c/generated/
-L/usr/local/lib/ -lzookeeper_mt
```

Before executing the program, let's create a few znodes in the ZooKeeper / root znode path using the ZooKeeper shell:

```
[zk: localhost(CONNECTED) 0] create /child1 ""
Created /child1
[zk: localhost(CONNECTED) 1] create /child2 ""
Created /child2
[zk: localhost(CONNECTED) 2] create /child3 ""
Created /child3
[zk: localhost(CONNECTED) 3] ls /
[child1, child3, zookeeper, child2]
[zk: localhost(CONNECTED) 4]
```

Now, let's try to list the znodes using the C client program that we have written, as shown in the following screenshot:

```
$ ./hello_zookeeper

: Client environment:zookeeper.version=zookeeper C client 3.4.6
: Client environment:host.name=ubuntu
: Client environment:os.name=Linux
: Client environment:os.arch=3.13.0-24-generic

: Initiating client connection, host=localhost:2181 sessionTimeout=2000 watcher=0x4007ed
  sessionId=0 sessionPasswd=<null> context=(nil) flags=0

: session establishment complete on server [127.0.0.1:2181], sessionId=0x1498d63efe30012,
  negotiated timeout=4000

  === znode listing === [ / ]
  (1): child1
  (2): child3
  (3): zookeeper
  (4): child2
  === done ===

: Closing zookeeper sessionId=0x1498d63efe30012 to [127.0.0.1:2181]
```

In the preceding output, we can see that as the C client executes, the client library displays a lot of informative log messages that pertain to the client library version, the operating system, and the architecture of the machine. Then, it tries to connect to the ZooKeeper server, and once connected, it prints the listing of znodes, which is the same as what we get through the ZooKeeper shell. Finally, it closes the session with the ZooKeeper server.

Example – the znode data watcher

In this section, we will implement a znode data-watcher client similar to what we did while reading about the ZooKeeper Java client APIs. To illustrate the znode data watcher, we will write a client zdata_watcher.c using the C APIs, which will continuously listen for ZOO_CHANGED_EVENT events from the ZooKeeper server in a znode path called /MyData. Another client program, zdata_updater.c, will periodically update the data field in /MyData, which will result in the generation of events, and upon receiving these events, zdata_watcher.c will print the changed data into the terminal.

Let's take a look at the source code of `zdata_watcher.c`:

```c
#include <stdio.h>
#include <errno.h>
#include <string.h>
#include <stdlib.h>
#include <unistd.h>
#include <zookeeper.h>

/* ZooKeeper Znode Data Length (1MB, the max supported) */
#define ZDATALEN    1024 * 1024
static char *host_port;
static char *zoo_path = "/MyData";
static zhandle_t *zh;
static int is_connected;
static char *watcher_ctx = "ZooKeeper Data Watcher";
/**
 * Watcher function for connection state change events
 */
void connection_watcher(zhandle_t *zzh, int type, int state,
    const char *path, void* context)
{
    if (type == ZOO_SESSION_EVENT)
    {
        if (state == ZOO_CONNECTED_STATE)
        {
            is_connected = 1;
        }
        else
        {
            is_connected = 0;
        }
    }
}
/**
 * Data Watcher function for /MyData node
 */
static void
data_watcher(zhandle_t *wzh, int type, int state, const char
    *zpath, void *watcher_ctx)
{
    char *zoo_data = malloc(ZDATALEN * sizeof(char));
    int zoo_data_len = ZDATALEN;

    if (state == ZOO_CONNECTED_STATE)
```

```
  {
    if (type == ZOO_CHANGED_EVENT)
    {
      /* Get the updated data and reset the watch */
      zoo_wget(wzh, zoo_path, data_watcher,
      (void *)watcher_ctx, zoo_data, &zoo_data_len, NULL);
      fprintf(stderr, "!!! Data Change Detected !!!\n");
      fprintf(stderr, "%s\n", zoo_data);
    }
  }
}

int main(int argc, char *argv[])
{
  int zdata_len;
  char *zdata_buf = NULL;

  if (argc != 2)
  {
    fprintf(stderr, "USAGE: %s host:port\n", argv[0]);
    exit(EXIT_FAILURE);
  }

  host_port = argv[1];

  zh = zookeeper_init(host_port, connection_watcher,
    2000, 0, 0, 0);

  if (zh == NULL)
  {
    fprintf(stderr,
      "Error connecting to ZooKeeper server[%d]!\n", errno);
    exit(EXIT_FAILURE);
  }

  while (1)
  {
    if (is_connected)
    {
      zdata_buf = (char *)malloc(ZDATALEN * sizeof(char));

      if (ZNONODE == zoo_exists(zh, zoo_path, 0, NULL))
      {
```

```
        if (ZOK == zoo_create( zh, zoo_path, NULL, -1,
          & ZOO_OPEN_ACL_UNSAFE, 0, NULL, 0))
        {
          fprintf(stderr, "%s created!\n", zoo_path);
        }
        else
        {
          fprintf(stderr,
          "Error Creating %s!\n", zoo_path);
          exit(EXIT_FAILURE);
        }
      }
      if (ZOK != zoo_wget(zh, zoo_path, data_watcher,
        watcher_ctx, zdata_buf, &zdata_len, NULL))
      {
        fprintf(stderr, "Error setting watch at %s!\n", zoo_path);
      }

      pause();
    }
  }

  free(zdata_buf);
  return 0;
}
```

The `zdata_updater` connects to the ZooKeeper instance that is running in the `localhost` and updates the data field of the znode path `/MyData` with the current local date and time. It updates the znode path `/MyData` every 5 seconds, which makes the ZooKeeper server to trigger an event of type `ZOO_CHANGED_EVENT`. The `zdata_watcher`, which had set a watch for this znode path, receives the notification for the data change event. It then retrieves the current data, resets the watch, and prints the data in the console.

The code for the data updater is illustrated next:

```
#include <time.h>
#include <stdio.h>
#include <errno.h>
#include <string.h>
#include <stdlib.h>
#include <unistd.h>
#include <zookeeper.h>
/* ZooKeeper Znode Data Length (1MB, the max supported) */
#define ZDATALEN    1024 * 1024
```

```
static char *host_port;
static char *zoo_path = "/MyData";

static zhandle_t *zh;
static int is_connected;

/**
* Watcher function for connection state change events
*/
void connection_watcher(zhandle_t *zzh, int type, int state,
  const char *path, void* context)
{
  if (type == ZOO_SESSION_EVENT)
  {
    if (state == ZOO_CONNECTED_STATE)
    {
      is_connected = 1;
    }
    else
    {
      is_connected = 0;
    }
  }
}

int main(int argc, char *argv[])
{
  char zdata_buf[128];
  struct tm *local;
  time_t t;

  if (argc != 2)
  {
    fprintf(stderr, "USAGE: %s host:port\n", argv[0]);
    exit(EXIT_FAILURE);
  }

  host_port = argv[1];

  zh = zookeeper_init(host_port, connection_watcher,
    2000, 0, 0, 0);

    if (zh == NULL)
```

```
    {
      fprintf(stderr,
        "Error connecting to ZooKeeper server[%d]!\n", errno);
      exit(EXIT_FAILURE);
    }

    sleep(3); /* Sleep a little for connection to complete */

    if (is_connected)
    {
      if (ZNONODE == zoo_exists(zh, zoo_path, 0, NULL))
      {
        fprintf(stderr, "%s doesn't exist! \
          Please start zdata_watcher.\n", zoo_path);
        exit(EXIT_FAILURE);
      }

      while(1)
      {
        t = time(NULL);
        local = localtime(&t);
        memset(zdata_buf,'\0',strlen(zdata_buf));
        strcpy(zdata_buf,asctime(local));

        if (ZOK != zoo_set(zh, zoo_path, zdata_buf,
          strlen(zdata_buf), -1))
        {
          fprintf(stderr, "Error in write at %s!\n", zoo_path);
        }

        sleep(5);
      }
    }

    return 0;
  }
}
```

Let's compile these two programs and see them in action:

```
$ gcc -Wall zdata_watcher.c -o zdata_watcher
-I${ZK_HOME}/src/c/include -I${ZK_HOME}/src/c/generated/
-L/usr/local/lib/ -lzookeeper_mt
$ gcc -Wall zdata_updater.c -o zdata_updater
-I${ZK_HOME}/src/c/include -I${ZK_HOME}/src/c/generated/
-L/usr/local/lib/ -lzookeeper_mt
```

In one terminal window, when you execute `zdata_watcher`, it creates a znode in the path `/MyData`, and starts listening for events of the type `ZOO_CHANGED_EVENT`:

```
$ ./zdata_watcher localhost:2181

: Initiating client connection, host=localhost:2181 sessionTimeout=2000 watcher=0x400
  9ed sessionId=0 sessionPasswd=<null> context=(nil) flags=0

: session establishment complete on server [127.0.0.1:2181], sessionId=0x1498d63efe300
  13, negotiated timeout=4000
  /MyData created!
```

Once we execute the `zdata_watcher`, it initiates a connection to the ZooKeeper server, and after the session is established, it creates a znode called `/MyData` in the root path of the ZooKeeper tree.

Now, in another terminal, when you run the `zdata_updater`, the `zdata_watcher` starts receiving the ZooKeeper events.

```
$ ./zdata_updater localhost:2181
```

After starting the `zdata_updater` client, you will see output similar to the following in the terminal window where the `zdata_watcher` is running:

```
!!! Data Change Detected !!!
Sat Nov  8 10:15:53 2014

!!! Data Change Detected !!!
Sat Nov  8 10:15:58 2014

!!! Data Change Detected !!!
Sat Nov  8 10:16:03 2014
```

Our data-watcher client is working successfully. From these examples, you will have a firm grasp on the ZooKeeper C client APIs. In these examples, we have used the synchronous APIs provided by the C APIs. However, in real applications, the asynchronous APIs are most commonly used. Implementation of the previous examples using the asynchronous API calls is left as an exercise for the readers. Also, it's recommended that you use the multithreaded version of the API. For example, with the single-threaded library, a callback might block a thread while performing other operations such as disk I/O, which might cause session timeout. The multithreaded library uses separate threads to handle callbacks, and this issue will not occur.

In the next section, we will learn about the ZooKeeper APIs for the Python programming language.

Python client bindings

Apache ZooKeeper is shipped with an official client binding for Python, which is developed on top of the C bindings. It can be found in the `contrib/zkpython` directory of the ZooKeeper distribution. To build and install the Python binding, refer to the instructions in the README file there. In this section, we will learn about another popular Python client library for ZooKeeper, called **Kazoo** (`https://kazoo.readthedocs.org/`).

Kazoo is a pure Python library for ZooKeeper, which means that, unlike the official Python bindings, Kazoo is implemented fully in Python and has no dependency on the C bindings of ZooKeeper. Along with providing both synchronous and asynchronous APIs, the Kazoo library also provides APIs for some distributed data structure primitives such as distributed locks, leader election, distributed queues, and so on.

Installation of Kazoo is very simple, which can be done either with `pip` or `easy_install` installers:

Using `pip`, Kazoo can be installed with the following command:

```
$ pip install kazoo
```

Using `easy_install`, Kazoo is installed as follows:

```
$ easy_install kazoo
```

To verify whether Kazoo is installed properly, let's try to connect to the ZooKeeper instance and print the list of znodes in the root path of the tree, as shown in the following screenshot:

```
$ python
Python 2.7.6 (default, Mar 22 2014, 22:59:56)
[GCC 4.8.2] on linux2
Type "help", "copyright", "credits" or "license" for more information.
>>> from kazoo.client import KazooClient
>>> zk = KazooClient(hosts='localhost:2181')
>>> zk.start()
>>> print zk.get_children('/')
[u'zookeeper']
>>>
>>> zk.stop()
>>>
```

In the preceding example, we imported the `KazooClient`, which is the main ZooKeeper client class. Then, we created an object of the class (an instance of KazooClient) by connecting to the ZooKeeper instance that is running on the localhost. Once we called the `start()` method, it initiates a connection to the ZooKeeper server.

Once successfully connected, the instance contains the handle to the ZooKeeper session. Now, when we called the `get_children()` method on the root path of the ZooKeeper namespace, it returned a list of the children. Finally, we closed the connection by calling the `stop()` method.

 Detailed documentation of the Kazoo Python library is available at `https://kazoo.readthedocs.org/en/latest/index.html`.

A watcher implementation

Kazoo provides a higher-level child and data-watching APIs as a recipe through a module called `kazoo.recipe.watchers`. This module provides the implementation of `DataWatch` and `ChildrenWatch` along with another class called `PatientChildrenWatch`. The `PatientChildrenWatch` class returns values after the children of a node don't change for a period of time, unlike the other two, which return each time an event is generated.

Let's look at the implementation of a simple children-watcher client, which will generate an event each time a znode is added or deleted from the ZooKeeper path:

```
import signal
from kazoo.client import KazooClient
from kazoo.recipe.watchers import ChildrenWatch
zoo_path = '/MyPath'
zk = KazooClient(hosts='localhost:2181')
zk.start()
zk.ensure_path(zoo_path)
@zk.ChildrenWatch(zoo_path)
def child_watch_func(children):
print "List of Children %s" % children
while True:
signal.pause()
```

In this simple implementation of a children watcher, we connect to the ZooKeeper server that is running in the localhost, using the following code, and create a path /MyPath:

```
zk.ensure_path(zoo_path)
@zk.ChildrenWatch(zoo_path)
```

We then set a children watcher on this path and register a callback method child_watch_func, which prints the current list of children on the event generated in /MyPath.

When we run this client watcher in a terminal, it starts listening to events:

```
$ python children_watcher.py
List of Children []
```

On another terminal, we will create some znodes in /MyPath with the ZooKeeper shell:

```
[zk: localhost(CONNECTED) 0] create /MyPath/child1 ""
Created /MyPath/child1
[zk: localhost(CONNECTED) 1] create /MyPath/child2 ""
Created /MyPath/child2
[zk: localhost(CONNECTED) 2] create /MyPath/child3 ""
Created /MyPath/child3
```

We observe that the children-watcher client receives these znode creation events, and it prints the list of the current children in the terminal window:

```
List of Children [u'child1']
List of Children [u'child1', u'child2']
List of Children [u'child1', u'child3', u'child2']
```

Similarly, if we delete the znodes that we just created, the watcher will receive the events and subsequently will print the children listing in the console:

```
[zk: localhost(CONNECTED) 3] delete /MyPath/child3
[zk: localhost(CONNECTED) 4] delete /MyPath/child2
[zk: localhost(CONNECTED) 5] delete /MyPath/child1
```

The messages shown in the following screenshot are printed in the terminal where the children watcher is running:

```
List of Children [u'child1', u'child2']
List of Children [u'child1']
List of Children []
```

Summary

In this chapter, we have learned how to write client programs for Apache ZooKeeper using three different languages: Java, C, and Python. We saw how to develop simple client code for connecting to a ZooKeeper server, implementation of watchers, and even more advanced use cases of development. It is recommended that you go through the API documentation of the individual client libraries so as to be well versed with the methods and constructs of each one of them.

In the next chapter, we will look into some advanced topics of ZooKeeper programming, where we will look at the algorithms and steps to implement common distributed system tasks such as leader election, group membership, and so on, using ZooKeeper primitives. We will also learn how to implement distributed data structures such as locks, barriers, and queues with ZooKeeper.

4

Performing Common Distributed System Tasks

In the previous chapter, you learned about the ZooKeeper client API and programming using the APIs. You saw how to write a client to connect to the ZooKeeper server instance and execute methods to carry out operations in the ZooKeeper namespace. You also learned how to implement watchers in a client so as to register for specific events and get notifications when such events occur, all in real time.

The simple yet powerful and elegant programming model of ZooKeeper enables us to implement high-level primitives for distributed systems. For example, we used the concept of ephemeral znodes to build an emulation of a cluster monitor in the previous chapter.

In this chapter, you will learn:

- How to carry out common distributed system tasks such as leader election, group memberships, and two-phase commit protocol
- How to implement a few distributed data structures such as barriers, locks, and queues

The high-level constructs outlined in this chapter are also known as ZooKeeper recipes. These are implemented on the client side using ZooKeeper's programming model and require no special support from the server side. Again, in the absence of ZooKeeper and its APIs, the implementation of these recipes would have been quite complex and difficult.

Some of the third-party and community-developed ZooKeeper client bindings also provide these high-level distributed systems' constructs as a part of their client library. For example, Netflix Curator, a feature-rich Java client framework for ZooKeeper, provides many of the recipes mentioned in this chapter. You will learn more about Curator later in this book. Kazoo, the Python client library that you learned in the previous chapter, also implements some of these recipes that developers can directly use in their client applications.

The ZooKeeper distribution is shipped with recipes for leader election and distributed lock and queue; these can be used inside distributed applications. The Java implementations for the three recipes can be found in the `recipes` folder of the distribution.

ZooKeeper recipes

In this section, you will learn to develop high-level distributed system constructs and data structures using ZooKeeper. As mentioned earlier, most of these constructs and functions are of utmost importance in building scalable distributed architectures, but they are fairly complicated to implement from scratch. Developers can often get bogged down while implementing these and integrating them with their application logic. In this section, you will learn how to develop algorithms to build some of these high-level functions using ZooKeeper's data model and primitives and see how ZooKeeper makes it simple, scalable, and error free, with much less code.

Barrier

Barrier is a type of synchronization method used in distributed systems to block the processing of a set of nodes until a condition is satisfied. It defines a point where all nodes must stop their processing and cannot proceed until all the other nodes reach this barrier.

The algorithm to implement a barrier using ZooKeeper is as follows:

1. To start with, a znode is designated to be a barrier znode, say `/zk_barrier`.
2. The barrier is said to be active in the system if this barrier znode exists.
3. Each client calls the ZooKeeper API's `exists()` function on `/zk_barrier` by registering for watch events on the barrier znode (the watch event is set to `true`).
4. If the `exists()` method returns `false`, the barrier no longer exists, and the client proceeds with its computation.
5. Else, if the `exists()` method returns `true`, the clients just waits for watch events.

6. Whenever the barrier exit condition is met, the client in charge of the barrier will delete `/zk_barrier`.

7. The deletion triggers a watch event, and on getting this notification, the client calls the `exists()` function on `/zk_barrier` again.

8. Step 7 returns `true`, and the clients can proceed further.

 The barrier exists until the barrier znode ceases to exist!

In this way, we can implement a barrier using ZooKeeper without much of an effort.

The example cited so far is for a simple barrier to stop a group of distributed processes from waiting on some condition and then proceed together when the condition is met. There is another type of barrier that aids in synchronizing the beginning and end of a computation; this is known as a double barrier. The logic of a double barrier states that a computation is started when the required number of processes join the barrier. The processes leave after completing the computation, and when the number of processes participating in the barrier become zero, the computation is stated to end.

The algorithm for a double barrier is implemented by having a `barrier` znode that serves the purpose of being a parent for individual process znodes participating in the computation. Its algorithm is outlined as follows:

Phase 1: Joining the `barrier` znode can be done as follows:

1. Suppose the `barrier` znode is represented by `znode/barrier`. Every client process registers with the `barrier` znode by creating an ephemeral znode with `/barrier` as the parent. In real scenarios, clients might register using their hostnames.

2. The client process sets a watch event for the existence of another znode called `ready` under the `/barrier` znode and waits for the node to appear.

3. A number N is predefined in the system; this governs the minimum number of clients to join the barrier before the computation can start.

4. While joining the barrier, each client process finds the number of child znodes of `/barrier`:

    ```
    M = getChildren(/barrier, watch=false)
    ```

5. If M is less than N, the client waits for the watch event registered in step 3.

6. Else, if M is equal to N, then the client process creates the `ready` znode under `/barrier`.

7. The creation of the ready znode in step 5 triggers the `watch` event, and each client starts the computation that they were waiting so far to do.

Phase 2: Leaving the `barrier` can be done as follows:

1. Client processing on finishing the computation deletes the znode it created under `/barrier` (in step 2 of Phase 1: Joining the barrier).

2. The client process then finds the number of children under `/barrier`:

```
M = getChildren(/barrier, watch=True)
```

If M is not equal to 0, this client waits for notifications (observe that we have set the watch event to `True` in the preceding call).

If M is equal to 0, then the client exits the `barrier` znode.

The preceding procedure suffers from a potential herd effect where all client processes wake up to check the number of children left in the barrier when a notification is triggered. To get away with this, we can use a sequential ephemeral znode to be created in step 2 of Phase 1: Joining the barrier. Every client process watches its next lowest sequential ephemeral znode to go away as an exit criterion. This way, only a single event is generated for any client completing the computation, and hence, not all clients need to wake up together to check on its exit condition. For a large number of client processes participating in a barrier, the herd effect can negatively impact the scalability of the ZooKeeper service, and developers should be aware of such scenarios.

 A Java language implementation of a double barrier can be found in the ZooKeeper documentation at `http://zookeeper.apache.org/doc/r3.4.6/zookeeperTutorial.html`.

Queue

A distributed queue is a very common data structure used in distributed systems. A special implementation of a queue, called a producer-consumer queue, is where a collection of processes called producers generate or create new items and put them in the queue, while consumer processes remove the items from the queue and process them. The addition and removal of items in the queue follow a strict ordering of FIFO.

A producer-consumer queue can be implemented using ZooKeeper. A znode will be designated to hold a queue instance, say queue-znode. All queue items are stored as znodes under this znode. Producers add an item to the queue by creating a znode under the queue-znode, and consumers retrieve the items by getting and then deleting a child from the queue-znode.

The FIFO order of the items is maintained using sequential property of znode provided by ZooKeeper. When a producer process creates a znode for a queue item, it sets the sequential flag. This lets ZooKeeper append the znode name with a monotonically increasing sequence number as the suffix. ZooKeeper guarantees that the sequence numbers are applied in order and are not reused. The consumer process processes the items in the correct order by looking at the sequence number of the znode.

The pseudocode for the algorithm to implement a producer-consumer queue using ZooKeeper is shown here:

1. Let /_QUEUE_ represent the top-level znode for our queue implementation, which is also called the queue-node.

2. Clients acting as producer processes put something into the queue by calling the `create()` method with the znode name as `"queue-"` and set the sequence and ephemeral flags if the `create()` method call is set `true`:

   ```
   create( "queue-", SEQUENCE_EPHEMERAL)
   ```

   The sequence flag lets the new znode get a name like `queue-N`, where *N* is a monotonically increasing number.

3. Clients acting as consumer processes process a `getChildren()` method call on the queue-node with a `watch` event set to `true`:

   ```
   M = getChildren(/_QUEUE_, true)
   ```

   It sorts the children list `M`, takes out the lowest numbered child znode from the list, starts processing on it by taking out the data from the znode, and then deletes it.

4. The client picks up items from the list and continues processing on them. On reaching the end of the list, the client should check again whether any new items are added to the queue by issuing another `get_children()` method call.

5. The algorithm continues when `get_children()` returns an empty list; this means that no more znodes or items are left under /_QUEUE_.

It's quite possible that in step 3, the deletion of a znode by a client will fail because some other client has gained access to the znode while this client was retrieving the item. In such scenarios, the client should retry the `delete` call.

Using this algorithm for implementation of a generic queue, we can also build a priority queue out of it, where each item can have a priority tagged to it. The algorithm and implementation is left as an exercise to the readers.

C and Java implementations of the distributed queue recipe are shipped along with the ZooKeeper distribution under the `recipes` folder. Developers can use this recipe to implement distributed lock in their applications.

Kazoo, the Python client library for ZooKeeper, has distributed queue implementations inside the `kazoo.recipe.queue` module. This queue implementation has priority assignment to the queue items support as well as the queue locking support that is built into it.

Lock

A lock in a distributed system is an important primitive that provides the applications with a means to synchronize their access to shared resources. Distributed locks need to be globally synchronous to ensure that no two clients can hold the same lock at any instance of time.

Typical scenarios where locks are inevitable are when the system as a whole needs to ensure that only one node of the cluster is allowed to carry out an operation at a given time, such as:

- Write to a shared database or file
- Act as a decision subsystem
- Process all I/O requests from other nodes

ZooKeeper can be used to implement mutually exclusive locks for processes that run on different servers across different networks and even geographically apart.

To build a distributed lock with ZooKeeper, a persistent znode is designated to be the main lock-znode. Client processes that want to acquire the lock will create an ephemeral znode with a sequential flag set under the lock-znode. The crux of the algorithm is that the lock is owned by the client process whose child znode has the lowest sequence number. ZooKeeper guarantees the order of the sequence number, as sequence znodes are numbered in a monotonically increasing order. Suppose there are three znodes under the lock-znode: *l1*, *l2*, and *l3*. The client process that created *l1* will be the owner of the lock. If the client wants to release the lock, it simply deletes *l1*, and then the owner of *l2* will be the lock owner, and so on.

The pseudocode for the algorithm to implement a distributed lock service with ZooKeeper is shown here:

Let the parent lock node be represented by a persistent znode, /_locknode_, in the Zookeeper tree.

Phase 1: Acquire a lock with the following steps:

1. Call the create("/_locknode_/lock-",CreateMode=EPHEMERAL_SEQUENTIAL) method.
2. Call the getChildren("/_locknode_/lock-", false) method on the lock node. Here, the watch flag is set to false, as otherwise it can lead to a herd effect.
3. If the znode created by the client in step 1 has the lowest sequence number suffix, then the client is owner of the lock, and it exits the algorithm.
4. Call the exists("/_locknode_/<znode path with next lowest sequence number>, True) method.
5. If the exists() method returns false, go to step 2.
6. If the exists() method returns true, wait for notifications for the watch event set in step 4.

Phase 2: Release a lock as follows:

1. The client holding the lock deletes the node, thereby triggering the next client in line to acquire the lock.
2. The client that created the next higher sequence node will be notified and hold the lock. The watch for this event was set in step 4 of Phase 1: Acquire a lock.

While it's not recommended that you use a distributed system with a large number of clients due to the herd effect, if the other clients also need to know about the change of lock ownership, they could set a watch on the /_locknode_ lock node for events of the NodeChildrenChanged type and can determine the current owner.

If there was a partial failure in the creation of znode due to connection loss, it's possible that the client won't be able to correctly determine whether it successfully created the child znode. To resolve such a situation, the client can store its session ID in the znode data field or even as a part of the znode name itself. As a client retains the same session ID after a reconnect, it can easily determine whether the child znode was created by it by looking at the session ID.

The idea of creating an ephemeral znode prevents a potential dead-lock situation that might arise when a client dies while holding a lock. However, as the property of the ephemeral znode dictates that it gets deleted when the session times out or expires, ZooKeeper will delete the znode created by the dead client, and the algorithm runs as usual. However, if the client hangs for some reason but the ZooKeeper session is still active, then we might get into a deadlock. This can be solved by having a monitor client that triggers an alarm when the lock holding time for a client crosses a predefined time out.

The ZooKeeper distribution is shipped with the C and Java language implementation of a distributed lock in the `recipes` folder. The recipe implements the algorithm you have learned so far and takes into account the problems associated with partial failure and herd effect.

The previous recipe of a mutually exclusive lock can be modified to implement a shared lock as well. Readers can find the algorithm and pseudocode for a shared lock using ZooKeeper in the documentation at `http://zookeeper.apache.org/doc/r3.4.6/recipes.html#Shared+Locks`.

Leader election

In distributed systems, leader election is the process of designating a single server as the organizer, coordinator, or initiator of some task distributed among several individual servers (nodes). After a leader election algorithm is run, a leader or a coordinator among the set of nodes is selected, and the algorithm must ascertain that all the nodes in the system acknowledge its candidature without any discrepancies for the correct functioning of the system.

A leader in a distributed system is required to act as a centralized controller of tasks that simplifies process synchronization. However, a centralized node is a single point of failure, and during failure, it can lead to an anomaly in the system. Hence, a correct and robust leader election algorithm is required to choose a new coordinator or leader on failure of the existing one.

A leader election algorithm has the following two required properties:

- **Liveness**: This ensures that most of the time, there is a leader
- **Safety**: This ensures that at any given time, there is either no leader or one leader

ZooKeeper can be used to implement a leader-election algorithm, and it can use this algorithm as a leader elector service in distributed applications. The algorithm is similar to the one we used to develop a global mutually-exclusive distributed lock.

Client processes nominating themselves as leaders use the SEQUENCE | EPHEMERAL flags when creating znodes under a parent znode. ZooKeeper automatically appends a monotonically increasing sequence number as a suffix to the child znode as the sequence flag is set. The process that created the znode with the smallest appended sequence number is elected as the leader. However, the algorithm should also take into account the failure of the leader.

The pseudocode for the algorithm is outlined here.

Let /_election_ be the election znode path that acts as the root for all clients participating in the leader election algorithm.

Clients with proposals for their nomination in the leader election procedure perform the following steps:

1. Create a znode with the /_election_/candidate-sessionID_ path, with both the SEQUENCE and EPHEMERAL flags. The sessionID identifier, as a part of the znode name, helps in recognizing znodes in the case of partial failures due to connection loss. Now, say that ZooKeeper assigns a sequence number N to the znode when the create() call succeeds.

2. Retrieve the current list of children in the election znode as follows:

    ```
    L = getChildren("/_election_", false)
    ```

    Here, L represents the list of children of "/_election_".

    The watch is set to false to prevent any herd effect.

3. Set a watch for changes in /_election_/candidate-sessionID_M, where M is the largest sequence number such that M is less than N, and candidate-sessionID_M is a znode in L as follows:

    ```
    exists("/_election_/candidate-sessionID_M", true)
    ```

4. Upon receiving a notification of znode deletion for the watches set in step 3, execute the getChildren(("/_election_", false) method on the election znode.

5. Let L be the new list of children of _election_. The leader is then elected as follows:

    1. If candidate-sessionID_N (this client) is the smallest node in L, then declare itself as the leader.

    2. Watch for changes on /_election_/candidate-sessionID_M, where M is the largest sequence number such that M is less than N and candidate-sessionID_M is a znode in L.

6. If the current leader crashes, the client having the znode with the next highest sequence number becomes the leader and so on.

Optionally, a persistent znode is also maintained where the client declaring itself as the leader can store its identifier so that other clients can query who the current leader is by reading this znode at any given time. Such a znode also ensures that that the newly elected leader has acknowledged and executed the leader election procedure correctly.

A Java language implementation for the leader election algorithm using ZooKeeper can be found in the `recipes` folder of the latest ZooKeeper distribution.

Group membership

A group membership protocol in a distributed system enables processes to reach a consensus on a group of processes that are currently alive and operational in the system. Membership protocols belong to the core components of a distributed system; they aid in maintaining service availability and consistency for the applications. It allows other processes to know when a process joins the system and leaves the system, thereby allowing the whole cluster to be aware of the current system state.

The implementation of a basic group membership protocol is very simple, and we have already used a variant of it while developing the cluster monitor emulation in *Chapter 3, Programming with Apache ZooKeeper*. A group membership protocol can be developed using the concept of ephemeral znodes. Any client that joins the cluster creates an ephemeral znode under a predefined path to locate memberships in the ZooKeeper tree and set a watch on the parent path. When another node joins or leaves the cluster, this node gets a notification and becomes aware of the change in the group membership.

The pseudocode for the algorithm to implement this group membership protocol is shown here.

Let a persistent znode, `/membership`, represent the root of the group in the ZooKeeper tree. A group membership protocol can then be implemented as follows:

1. Clients joining the group create ephemeral nodes under the group root to indicate membership.

2. All the members of the group will register for watch events on /membership, thereby being aware of other members in the group. This is done as shown in the following code:

```
L = getChildren("/membership", true)
```

3. When a new client arrives and joins the group, all other members are notified.

4. Similarly, when a client leaves due to failure or otherwise, ZooKeeper automatically deletes the ephemeral znodes created in step 2. This triggers an event, and other group members get notified.

5. Live members know which node joined or left by looking at the list of children L.

The preceding algorithm suffers from the herd effect, as events of NodeChildrenChanged emitted due to the joining or leaving of members will cause all other members to wake up and find the current membership of the system.

Two-phase commit

The **two-phase commit** (2PC) protocol is a distributed algorithm that coordinates all the processes that participate in a distributed atomic transaction on whether to commit or abort (roll back) the transaction. 2PC is a specialized type of consensus protocol and is widely used in transaction processing systems. It ensures an atomic behavior that guarantees that either all the transactions or none of them are completed so that the resources under transactional control remain synchronized.

The **2PC** protocol consists of two phases, which are as follows:

- In the first phase, the coordinator node asks all the transaction's participating processes to prepare and vote to either commit or abort the transaction.

- In the second phase, the coordinator decides whether to commit or abort the transaction, depending on the result of the voting in the first phase. If all participants voted for commit, it commits the transaction; otherwise, it aborts it. It finally notifies the result to all the participants.

The **2PC** protocol is depicted in the following diagram:

We can develop a 2PC protocol implementation using ZooKeeper.

Let /2PC_Transactions represent the root node to run the 2PC algorithm in ZooKeeper. The algorithm to do so is as follows.

1. A coordinator node creates a transaction znode, say /2PC_Transactions/ TX. We can use the leader election algorithm to elect the coordinator using ZooKeeper. The coordinator node sets a watch on the transaction node.

2. Another persistent znode, tx_result, is created under /2PC_Transactions/ TX by the coordinator to post the result of the protocol, commit, or abort, and any additional outcomes of the transactions.

3. Each participating client node sets a watch on the /2PC_Transactions as well as /2PC_Transactions/TX/tx_result znode paths.

4. When the coordinator node creates the transaction znode, it notifies the participating client nodes that the coordinator node is requesting for voting on the transaction.

5. The participants then create an ephemeral child znode in the /2PC_Transactions/TX path, with their own identifier (say hostnames) and vote for commit or abort by writing to the data field of their specific znodes.

6. The coordinator is notified of the creation of all the child znodes, and when the number of child znodes in /2PC_Transactions/TX equals the number of participants, it checks the votes of all the participants by reading the participants' znodes.

7. If all the participants voted for commit, the coordinator commits the transaction; otherwise, it aborts it. Subsequently, it posts the result of the transaction by writing to the /2PC_Transactions/TX/tx_result znode.

8. The participant znodes get to know the outcome of the transaction when it gets a notification of NodeDataChanged for /2PC_Transactions/TX/tx_result.

The preceding algorithm might be a little slow, as all messaging happens through the coordinator node, but it takes care of the participant nodes' failure during the execution of the protocol, using ephemeral znodes.

Service discovery

Service discovery is one of the key components of distributed systems and service-oriented architectures where services need to find each other. In the simplest way, service discovery helps clients determine the IP and port for a service that exists on multiple hosts. One common example of this is how a web service can find the right host that serves a caching service in the network. At first glance, it appears that we can use a **Domain Name System** (DNS) service as a service discovery system. However, a solution with DNS is not viable when the service locations change frequently due to auto or manual scaling, new deployments of services, or when services are failed over or replaced with newer hosts due to host failures.

Important properties of a service discovery system are mentioned here:

- It allows services to register their availability
- It provides a mechanism to locate a live instance of a particular service
- It propagates a service change notification when the instances of a service change

Let /services represent the base path in the ZooKeeper tree for services of the system or platform. Persistent znodes under /services designate services available to be consumed by clients.

A simple service discovery model with ZooKeeper is illustrated as follows:

- Service registration: For service registrations, hosts that serve a particular service create an ephemeral znode in the relevant path under /services. For example, if a server is hosting a web-caching service, it creates an ephemeral znode with its hostname in /services/web_cache. Again, if some other server hosts a file-serving service, it creates another ephemeral znode with its hostname in /services/file_server and so on.

- Service discovery: Now, clients joining the system, register for watches in the znode path for the particular service. If a client wants to know the servers in the infrastructure that serve a web-caching service, the client will keep a watch in /services/web_cache.

  If a new host is added to serve web caching under this path, the client will automatically know the details about the new location. Again, if an existing host goes down, the client gets the event notification and can take the necessary action of connecting to another host.

A service discovery system provides a seamless mechanism to guarantee service continuity in the case of failures and is an indispensable part of building a robust and scalable distributed platform. Apache Curator provides an extension called curator-x-discovery in its ZooKeeper library; this implements a service registration and discovery model. It also provides a service discovery server called curator-x-discovery-server that exposes a RESTful web service to register, remove, and query services for non-Java or legacy applications to use the service discovery functionalities.

Summary

In this chapter, you saw how to implement high-level constructs of distributed systems using the ZooKeeper data model and primitives provided to it by its APIs. You learned the algorithms to develop important distributed data structures such as barrier, lock, and queue with ZooKeeper. We also studied the algorithms and looked at the pseudocode to implement some of the common tasks required in the development of distributed applications, namely leader election, group membership, and the 2PC protocol. You saw how we can solve these problems in a simple and lucid manner with ZooKeeper. While implementing the recipes, you also learned how to avoid some of the problems such as the herd effect and race conditions.

Developers should be careful when looking at these issues while developing their applications with ZooKeeper, as otherwise, the scalability of ZooKeeper gets negatively impacted, and it also leads to bursts of traffic in the network, thus causing service downgrade.

In the next chapter, we will read about configuration and administration of ZooKeeper in more detail. It's very important to learn about the various knobs and parameters to configure a ZooKeeper cluster so as to make the best use of it. We will also look at some of the best practices that developers and administrators should keep in mind while dealing with ZooKeeper in a production environment.

5
Administering Apache ZooKeeper

In the previous chapter on ZooKeeper recipes, you learned how to implement high-level constructs of distributed systems using ZooKeeper. We saw how ZooKeeper's data model, APIs, and its primitives drastically simplify implementation of these higher-order functions to a great extent. However, to get the best out of ZooKeeper in the distributed applications where it's used, we need to know to configure it properly and to know the various parameters that govern its functioning. Although ZooKeeper has been designed to be simple to use and to be operated on by both developers and distributed system administrators, a misconfigured ZooKeeper service might negatively impact the functioning of the applications. Hence, it's of the utmost importance that we know how to correctly configure, manage, and administer a ZooKeeper service that will help in diagnosing issues in a production environment.

In this chapter, we will study in detail how to configure and administer a ZooKeeper service instance. The following topics will be covered while we discuss ZooKeeper configuration and administration:

- Configuration of a ZooKeeper server
- Configuration of a ZooKeeper ensemble
- Configuration of quotas and authorizations
- Best practices for ZooKeeper
- Monitoring a ZooKeeper service

A detailed description of the ZooKeeper deployment and administration can found in the official documentation at `http://zookeeper.apache.org/doc/trunk/zookeeperAdmin.html`.

Configuring a ZooKeeper server

In this section, we will look at the various configuration parameters of a ZooKeeper server. These parameters are defined in the configuration file called `zoo.cfg`. Servers deployed in a ZooKeeper service can share a file if they are configured for the same applications. You have already learned about the `myid` file that distinguishes the servers from one another in the same ensemble. While the default options in this configuration file usually serve most common use cases for the evaluation or testing of applications, in a production environment it's very important that the values for these parameters are set properly with adequate reasoning.

It's also possible to set many of the configuration parameters using Java system properties with `zookeeper.propertyName`. These properties are set using the `-D` option when starting the server. However, parameters defined in the configuration file have precedence over the ones set with `-D` options in the Java command line.

Minimum configuration

The basic configuration parameters that must be defined in the configuration file for every ZooKeeper server are mentioned here. These parameters are not predefined and must be set in the configuration file to run a ZooKeeper instance. You already learned about these options in *Chapter 1, A Crash Course in Apache ZooKeeper*; they are presented here as a recap:

- `clientPort`: This is the TCP port where clients can connect to the server. The client port can be set to any number, and different servers can be configured to listen on different ports. The default port is 2181.

- `dataDir`: This is the directory where ZooKeeper will store the in-memory database snapshots. If the `dataLogDir` parameter is not defined separately, the transaction logs of updates to the database would also be stored in this directory. The `myid` file would also be stored in this directory if this server is a member of an ensemble. The data directory is not very performance-sensitive and is not required to be configured in a dedicated device if transaction logs are stored in a different location.

- `tickTime`: This is the length of a single tick measured in milliseconds. Tick is the basic time unit used by ZooKeeper to determine heartbeats and session timeouts. The default `tickTime` parameter is 2,000 milliseconds. Lowering the `tickTime` parameter enables quicker timeouts but increases network traffic (heartbeats) and processing overhead for the ZooKeeper server.

Storage configuration

In this section, we will look at some of the advanced parameters used to configure the storage options of a ZooKeeper server:

- `dataLogDir`: This is the directory where the ZooKeeper transaction logs are stored. The server flushes the transaction logs using sync writes. Hence, it's very important that a dedicated transaction log device be used so that transaction logging by the ZooKeeper server is not impacted by I/O activities from other processes in the system. Having a dedicated log device improves the overall throughput and assigns stable latencies to requests.

- `preAllocSize`: The `zookeeper.preAllocSize` Java system property is set to preallocate the block size to the transactions log files. The default block size is 64 MB. Preallocating the transaction log minimizes the disk seeks. If snapshots are taken frequently, the transaction logs might not grow to 64 MB. In such cases, we can tune this parameter to optimize the storage usage.

- `snapCount`: The `zookeeper.snapCount` Java system property gives us the number of transactions between two consecutive snapshots. After `snapCount` transactions are written to a logfile, a new snapshot is started, and a new transaction logfile is created. Snapshot is a performance-sensitive operation, and hence, having a smaller value for `snapCount` might negatively affect ZooKeeper's performance. The default value of `snapCount` parameter is 100,000.

- `traceFile`: The `requestTraceFile` Java system property sets this option to enable the logging of requests to a trace file named `traceFile.year.month.day`. This option is useful for debugging, but it impacts the overall performance of the ZooKeeper server.

- `fsync.warningthresholdms`: This is the time measured in milliseconds; it defines a threshold for the maximum amount of time permitted to flush all outstanding writes to the transactional log, **write-ahead log (WAL)**. It issues a warning message to the debug log whenever the sync operation takes longer than this value. The default value is 1,000.

- `autopurge.snapRetainCount`: This refers to the number of snapshots and corresponding transaction logs to retain in directories, `dataDir` and `dataLogDir`, respectively. The default value is 3.

- `autopurge.purgeInterval`: This refers to the time interval in hours to purge old snapshots and transaction logs. The default value is 0, which means auto purging is disabled by default. We can set this option to a positive integer (1 and above) to enable the auto purging. If it is disabled (set to 0), the default, purging doesn't happen automatically. Manual purging can be done by running the `zkCleanup.sh` script available in the `bin` directory of the ZooKeeper distribution.

- `syncEnabled`: This configuration option is newly introduced in 3.4.6 and later versions of ZooKeeper. It is set using the Java system property `zookeeper.observer.syncEnabled` to enable the "observers" to log transaction and write snapshot to disk, by default, like the "followers". Recall that observers do not participate in the voting process unlike followers, but commit proposals from the leader. Enabling this option reduces the recovery time of the observers on restart. The default value is `true`.

Network configuration

The configuration parameters discussed in this section relate to the clients' interaction with a ZooKeeper server:

- `globalOutstandingLimit`: This parameter defines the maximum number of outstanding requests in ZooKeeper. In real life, clients might submit requests faster than ZooKeeper can process them. This happens if there are a large number of clients. This parameter enables ZooKeeper to do flow control by throttling clients. This is done to prevent ZooKeeper from running out of memory due to the queued requests. ZooKeeper servers will start throttling client requests once the `globalOutstandingLimit` has been reached. The default limit is `1000` requests.

  (Java system property: `zookeeper.globalOutstandingLimit`)

- `maxClientCnxns`: This is the maximum number of concurrent socket connections between a single client and the ZooKeeper server. The client is identified by its IP address. Setting up a TCP connection is a resource-intensive operation, and this parameter is used to prevent the overloading of the server. It is also used to prevent certain classes of **DoS** attacks, including file descriptor exhaustion. The default value is `60`. Setting this to `0` entirely removes the limit on concurrent connections.

- `clientPortAddress`: This is the IP address that listens for client connections. By default, ZooKeeper server binds to all the interfaces for accepting client connection.

- `minSessionTimeout`: This is the minimum session timeout in milliseconds that the server will allow the client to negotiate. The default value is twice the `tickTime` parameter. If this timeout is set to a very low value, it might result in false positives due to incorrect detection of client failures. Setting this timeout to a higher value will delay the detection of client failures.

- `maxSessionTimeout`: This is the maximum session timeout in milliseconds that the server will allow the client to negotiate. By default, it is `20` times the `tickTime` parameter.

Configuring a ZooKeeper ensemble

In this section, we will look at configuration options that are mostly used with an ensemble of ZooKeeper servers. A ZooKeeper ensemble or cluster of replicated ZooKeeper servers should be configured optimally to avoid scenarios such as split-brain. A split-brain scenario might happen due to network portioning where two different servers of the same ensemble might pose as leaders and cause inconsistencies.

The following configuration options are available with an ensemble of ZooKeeper servers:

- `electionAlg`: This option is used to choose a leader in a ZooKeeper ensemble. A value of 0 corresponds to the original UDP-based version, 1 corresponds to the non-authenticated UDP-based version of fast leader election, 2 corresponds to the authenticated UDP-based version of fast leader election, and 3 corresponds to the TCP-based version of fast leader election. Currently, algorithm 3 is the default. The implementations of leader election 0, 1, and 2 are now deprecated, and fast leader election is the only one used. Available options are as follows

- `initLimit`: This refers to the amount of time, measured in ticks, to allow followers to connect with the leader. `initLimit` should be set depending on the network speed (and hops) between the leader and follower and based on the amount of data to be transferred between the two. If the amount of data stored by ZooKeeper is huge due to a large number of znodes and the amount of data stored in them, or if the network bandwidth is low, `initLimit` should be increased.

- `syncLimit`: This is the amount of time measured in ticks to allow followers to sync with a leader. If the followers fall too far behind the leader due to server load or network problems, they are dropped. However, the amount of data stored by ZooKeeper has no effect on the synchronization time between the leader and follower. Instead, `syncLimit` depends on network latency and throughput.

- `leaderServes`: By default, the server in an ensemble that runs in the leader mode also accepts client connections. However, in a loaded and busy ensemble with an update-heavy workload, we can configure the leader server to not accept client connections. This can be configured using the `zookeeper.leaderServes` Java system property. This can aid in coordinating write updates at a faster rate and, hence, can lead to increased write throughput.

- `cnxTimeout`: This refers to the timeout value for opening connections for leader election notifications. This parameter is only applicable with leader election algorithm 3 – `fast leader election`. The default value is 5 seconds.

- `server.x=[hostname]:port1[:port2]`: This parameter is used to define servers in the ZooKeeper ensemble. When the ZooKeeper server process starts up, it determines its identity by looking for the `myid` file in the data directory. The `myid` file contains the server number in ASCII; this should be the same as x in `server.x` of the configuration parameter. This parameter can be further explained as follows:

    ◦ There are two TCP port numbers: `port1` and `port2`. The first port is used to send transaction updates, and the second one is for leader election. The leader election port is only necessary if `electionAlg` is 1, 2, or 3 (default). In *Chapter 1, A Crash Course in Apache ZooKeeper*, we saw how to use different port numbers to test multiple servers on a single machine.

    ◦ It is very important that all servers use the same `server.x` configuration for proper connection to happen between them. Also, the list of servers that make up ZooKeeper servers that is used by the clients must match the list of ZooKeeper servers that each ZooKeeper server has.

Configuring a quorum

ZooKeeper allows for the flexible configuration of quorums within the ensemble. We can form hierarchical quorums by classifying the ZooKeeper servers into groups. This is particularly useful for forming a ZooKeeper ensemble that spans multiple data centers. An ensemble across data centers helps in ensuring a high availability of the service during disaster scenarios. The following options are useful for forming such groups in an ensemble:

- `group.x=nnnnn[:nnnnn]`: This enables a hierarchical quorum construction. x is a group identifier and *nnnnn* corresponds to server identifiers. Groups must be disjoint, and the union of all the groups must be the ZooKeeper ensemble.

- `weight.x=nnnnn`: This is used to assign weight to servers in a group when forming quorums. It corresponds to the weight of a server when voting for leader election and for the atomic broadcast protocol **Zookeeper Atomic Broadcast (ZAB)**. By default, the weight of a server is 1. Assigning more weight to a server allows it to form a quorum with other servers more easily.

Quota and authorization

ZooKeeper has configurable quotas associated with its data model. It's possible to set the quota limit on the znodes and the data amount of data stored. If a subtree in the ZooKeeper namespace crosses the quota associated with it, ZooKeeper prints warning messages in the log. However, the operation is never cancelled if the quota assigned is exceeded.

ZooKeeper quotas are stored in the ZooKeeper tree in the /zookeeper/quota path. It is possible to set, list, and delete quotas from the ZooKeeper client APIs and through the ZooKeeper Java shell. The following screenshot shows the results of using the set, list, and del commands:

```
[zk: localhost(CONNECTED) 0] create /quota_example ""
Created /quota_example
[zk: localhost(CONNECTED) 1] setquota -n 2 /quota_example
Comment: the parts are option -n val 2 path /quota_example
[zk: localhost(CONNECTED) 2] listquota /quota_example
absolute path is /zookeeper/quota/quota_example/zookeeper_limits
Output quota for /quota_example count=2,bytes=-1
Output stat for /quota_example count=1,bytes=2
[zk: localhost(CONNECTED) 3] create /quota_example/child1 ""
Created /quota_example/child1
[zk: localhost(CONNECTED) 4] create /quota_example/child2 ""
Created /quota_example/child2
[zk: localhost(CONNECTED) 5] create /quota_example/child3 ""
Created /quota_example/child3
[zk: localhost(CONNECTED) 6] ls /quota_example
[child1, child3, child2]
[zk: localhost(CONNECTED) 7] delquota /quota_example
[zk: localhost(CONNECTED) 8] listquota /quota_example
absolute path is /zookeeper/quota/quota_example/zookeeper_limits
quota for /quota_example does not exist.
[zk: localhost(CONNECTED) 9] _
```

In the preceding example, we created a new znode called /quota_example and set a quota of two child znodes. We then did a listing of the assigned quota and also saw how to delete the assigned quota.

When we created the third child under /quota_example, the following log message is printed as a warning in the ZooKeeper logfile, informing us that we have exceeded the quota:

```
WARN  [SyncThread:0:DataTree@388] - Quota exceeded: /quota_example count=3 limit=2
```

ZooKeeper also provides configurable options to control authentication and authorization by the service.

A `zookeeper.DigestAuthenticationProvider.superDigest` parameter enables a ZooKeeper ensemble administrator to access the znode hierarchy as a superuser. The ZooKeeper service doesn't do any ACL checking for a user who is authenticated as a superuser. This feature is disabled by default.

To generate a super digest for the superuser, the Java system property called `org.apache.zookeeper.server.auth.DigestAuthenticationProvider` can be used by calling with the parameter `super:<password>`. Once the `superDigest` is generated, we need to provide `super:<data>` as a system property while starting the ZooKeeper servers.

A ZooKeeper client need to pass a scheme of digest and authentication data of `super:<password>` to authenticate with the ZooKeeper server. While using the ZooKeeper shell, we can use the `addauth` command.

ZooKeeper best practices

Some of the best practices of running and managing a ZooKeeper ensemble are show here:

- The ZooKeeper data directory contains the snapshot and transactional log files. It is a good practice to periodically clean up the directory if the autopurge option is not enabled. Also, an administrator might want to keep a backup of these files, depending on the application needs. However, since ZooKeeper is a replicated service, we need to back up the data of only one of the servers in the ensemble.

- ZooKeeper uses Apache log4j as its logging infrastructure. As the logfiles grow bigger in size, it is recommended that you set the auto-rollover of the logfiles using the in-built log4j feature for ZooKeeper logs.

- The list of ZooKeeper servers used by the clients in their connection strings must match the list of ZooKeeper servers that each ZooKeeper server has. Strange behaviors might occur if the lists don't match.

- The server lists in each Zookeeper server configuration file should be consistent with the other members of the ensemble.

- As already mentioned, the ZooKeeper transaction log must be configured in a dedicated device. This is very important to achieve best performance from ZooKeeper.

- The Java heap size should be chosen with care. Swapping should never be allowed to happen in the ZooKeeper server. It is better if the ZooKeeper servers have a reasonably high memory (RAM).
- System monitoring tools such as `vmstat` can be used to monitor virtual memory statistics and decide on the optimal size of memory needed, depending on the need of the application. In any case, swapping should be avoided.

Monitoring a ZooKeeper instance

The ZooKeeper service can be monitored in the following two ways:

- Monitoring of health and status using a set of four-letter words
- Using Java Management Extensions capabilities built into ZooKeeper

Four-letter words

ZooKeeper responds to a small set of commands, each being composed of four letters. These commands can be issued through **telnet** or **nc** at the client port. The main objective of these commands is to provide a simple mechanism to check health of the server or diagnose any problems.

The following are the four-letter words supported by ZooKeeper services at the time of writing this book:

- `conf`: This print details about server configuration parameters such as `clientPort, dataDir, tickTime,` and so on.
- `cons`: This lists the full connection/session details for all clients connected to this server.
- `crst`: This resets connection/session statistics for all connections.
- `dump`: This lists the outstanding sessions and ephemeral nodes. This only works on the leader.
- `envi`: Lists the environment parameters
- `ruok`: This checks whether the server is running without any error. The server will respond with `imok` if it is running. If the server is in some error state, it will not respond to this command.
- `srst`: This resets the server statistics.
- `stat`: This provides information on the current status of the server and the list of connected clients.

- `srvr`: This provides the same information as the stat command, except the list of connected clients.

- `wchs`: This provides brief information on watches for the server.

- `wchc`: This provides detailed information on watches for the server, sorted by sessions (connections), showing a list of sessions with associated watches (paths).

- `wchp`: This provides detailed information on watches for the server, sorted by paths (znodes). This shows a list of paths with associated sessions.

- `mntr`: This outputs a list of variables that can be used to monitor the health of the cluster.

Some examples of running these four-letter commands to monitor the current status of the ZooKeeper server are shown in this screenshot:

```
$ echo ruok | nc localhost 2181
imok$
$
$ echo stat | nc localhost 2181
Zookeeper version: 3.4.6-1569965, built on 02/20/2014 09:09 GMT
Clients:
 /127.0.0.1:39906[0](queued=0,recved=1,sent=0)

Latency min/avg/max: 0/2/63
Received: 634
Sent: 633
Connections: 1
Outstanding: 0
Zxid: 0x299
Mode: standalone
Node count: 8
$
$ echo conf | nc localhost 2181
clientPort=2181
dataDir=/var/lib/zookeeper/version-2
dataLogDir=/var/lib/zookeeper/version-2
tickTime=2000
maxClientCnxns=60
minSessionTimeout=4000
maxSessionTimeout=40000
serverId=0
$
```

Java Management Extensions

ZooKeeper provides for extensive monitoring and management capabilities with **Java Management Extensions (JMX)**. In this section, we will look at using **jconsole**, a simple management console available with JMX, to explore ZooKeeper management.

Setting up of JMX for monitoring and management is beyond the scope of this book. For more details, visit https://docs.oracle.com/javase/7/docs/technotes/ guides/management/agent.html.

Now, let's start **jconsole** from the command line on the same system where ZooKeeper is also running. In our case, the ZooKeeper service is running on localhost. Running jconsole starts a window similar to the one shown in the following screenshot:

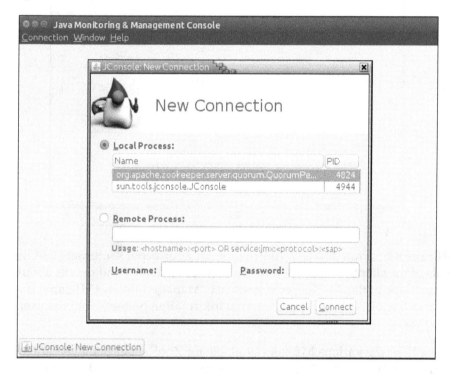

We can see that the ZooKeeper process with PID 4824 is discovered by jconsole. Let's connect to this process by double-clicking on it. Once jconsole attaches to the ZooKeeper process, we will see a window similar to the following one with various forms of system statistics, such as memory usage, thread, JVM-specific information, and so on. These statistics and system counters are very important to monitor the state of the ZooKeeper server and to help in debugging performance issues in a production cluster.

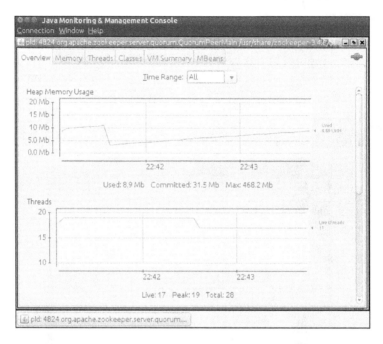

The **MBeans** tab shows detailed information on ZooKeeper's internal state, such as details of the clients connected and the various attributes and details about operations done in the ZooKeeper namespace. **Managed Beans** (**MBeans**) is a very elegant and flexible way to expose internal information on the ZooKeeper server through **JMX**.

More details on the various **MBeans** available for ZooKeeper management and monitoring can be found at `https://zookeeper.apache.org/doc/trunk/zookeeperJMX.html`.

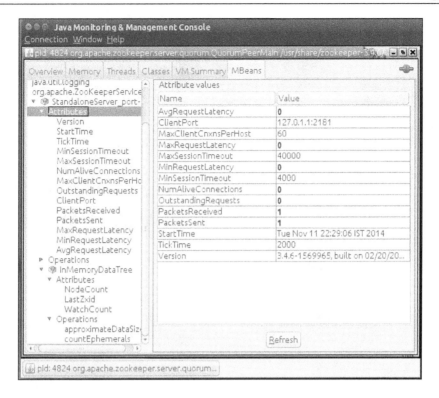

Summary

In this chapter, you learned in detail about the various configuration options of ZooKeeper that are an essential part of using and operating ZooKeeper. You also learned the various best practices of using ZooKeeper, followed by methods of monitoring and managing ZooKeeper servers in real time. Knowing the various knobs of ZooKeeper configuration is very important for production deployment and can help prevent many problems, which might be hard to debug later.

In the next chapter, you will learn about Curator, which is a high-level framework for Apache ZooKeeper. Curator is a set of wrapper libraries built on top of ZooKeeper with a lot of enhanced features and capabilities. Originally developed by Netflix, Curator is now an Apache project and is very popular among ZooKeeper users.

6

Decorating ZooKeeper with Apache Curator

So far in this book, we have studied Apache ZooKeeper in detail, from theoretical concepts to its programming. We have read and understood how ZooKeeper can be used in distributed systems to solve common and important tasks in a simple and neat way. We also looked into the administration aspects, and you saw how to configure ZooKeeper to get the best out of it in production systems.

Apache ZooKeeper is one among those software tools that aids in solving complex problems by relieving users from the intricacies of implementing them from scratch. However, ZooKeeper exposes only the primitives, and it's up to the users how they use these primitives to work out the coordination problems in their applications. To prevent users further from the involutions of using ZooKeeper, there have been numerous efforts in the community to develop high-level frameworks on top of the ZooKeeper data model and its APIs. **Apache Curator** is a high-level wrapper library and framework that makes ZooKeeper very simple and easy to use.

In this chapter, we will read about Curator and discuss the following topics:

- Curator and its components
- The Curator ZooKeeper client
- The Curator framework
- Curator recipes for ZooKeeper
- Netflix Exhibitor

 Curator was originally developed by Netflix and is now an Apache project. The project page is located at http://curator.apache.org/.

Curator components

Curator is a high-level library for ZooKeeper; it makes dealing with ZooKeeper much easier and it extends the functionality of core ZooKeeper. At a high level, Curator is composed of the following components:

- **Client**: The Curator client is a wrapper around ZooKeeper's Java client. It's a low-level API in the curator stack and abstracts functionalities out of the ZooKeeper client.

- **Framework**: The Curator framework is a high-level API with advanced features such as automatic connection management, retrying of operations, and so on. It simplifies the usage of ZooKeeper to a great extent.

- **Recipes**: The Curator recipes provide implementations of ZooKeeper recipes; these implementations can be directly used in distributed applications to solve coordination problems.

- **Extensions**: The Curator recipes package implements the common recipes. To avoid bloating this package, a separate extension package is used.

In addition to the preceding components, Curator also ships with a bunch of useful utilities for ZooKeeper. The Curator stack is shown in the following diagram:

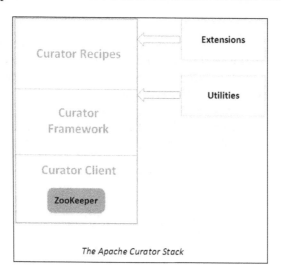

The Apache Curator Stack

The Curator JARs are available in repositories of Maven Central. Curator can be easily included in the build scripts of Maven, Gradle, Ivy, SBT, and so on.

The various Maven artifacts are listed at `http://mvnrepository.com/artifact/org.apache.curator`.

Curator client

Curator Client is a wrapper around ZooKeeper's Java client. It makes client access to ZooKeeper much simpler and less error-prone.

The curator client provides the following capabilities:

- **Connection management**: This manages the connection to the ZooKeeper server
- **Operations retry utilities**: This is a mechanism to retry operations
- **Test ZooKeeper server**: This is a ZooKeeper test server for testing

A sample code fragment of the `MyCuratorClient.java` file to connect to the ZooKeeper server with the curator client is shown as follows:

```
public void myCuratorClient() throws Exception
{
  CuratorZookeeperClient client =
  new CuratorZookeeperClient(server.getConnectString(),
    10000, 10000, null,new RetryOneTime(1));
  client.start();
  try
  {
    client.blockUntilConnectedOrTimedOut();
    String path = client.getZooKeeper().create("/test_znode",
    "".getBytes(),ZooDefs.Ids.OPEN_ACL_UNSAFE,
      CreateMode.PERSISTENT);
  }
  finally
  {
    client.close();
  }
}
```

The `CuratorZooKeeperClient` constructor is used to connect to the ZooKeeper server. It takes a connection string or a list of ZooKeeper host-port pairs, the session and connection timeout, an optional watcher object, and the retry policy to use. A retry policy is a mechanism for the client to try various retry mechanisms while retrying connections. In the preceding example, we used a policy where the client will retry only once.

The Curator client supports the following retry policies:

- **BoundedExponentialBackoffRetry**: This retries a specified number of times by increasing the sleep time between the retries up to a maximum upper bound

- **ExponentialBackoffRetry**: This retries a specified number of times by increasing the sleep time between the retries

- **RetryNTimes**: This retries *n* number of times

- **RetryOneTime**: This retries only once

- **RetryUntilElapsed**: This retries until a specified timeout has elapsed

Once the client is started, the `blockUntilConnectedOrTimedOut` method blocks until the connection to the ZooKeeper server succeeds or the connection timeout has elapsed. Once the connection succeeds, we will create a znode named `/test_znode`. The `getZooKeeper()` method returns the instance of the connection to the managed ZooKeeper server.

 The Curator API doc is available at `http://curator.apache.org/apidocs/index.html`.

The Curator client is a low-level API that gives an abstraction over the ZooKeeper client APIs. Developers should use the Curator framework instead of directly using the `CuratorZookeeperClient` class in their applications as a recommended practice.

Curator framework

The Curator framework (`org.apache.curator.framework`) is a high-level API that simplifies using ZooKeeper to a great extent. Some of the features it provides are as follows:

- **Automatic Connection Management**: This feature automatically and transparently handles the scenarios where clients need to recreate a connection to the ZooKeeper server and/or retry operations.

- **Simple and Flexible APIs**: This feature applies the raw ZooKeeper API with a set of modern, fluent interfaces.

- **Recipes**: This feature implements common ZooKeeper recipes. We will discuss them in the next section.

`CuratorFramework` is allocated using `CuratorFrameworkFactory`. It provides the factory methods as well as a builder to create instances. `CuratorFramework` instances are fully thread-safe. While developing applications using `CuratorFramework`, developers should create and share one `CuratorFramework` instance for every ZooKeeper cluster. The `CuratorFramework` uses a fluent-style interface.

A sample ZooKeeper client using `CuratorFramework` is shown in the following code snippet:

```
public void myCuratorFrameworkClient()
throws Exception
{
  CuratorFramework client =
  CuratorFrameworkFactory.newClient(server.getConnectString(),
    new RetryOneTime(1));
  client.start();
  try
  {
    String path = client.create().withMode(
    CreateMode.PERSISTENT).forPath(
    "/test_znode", "".getBytes());
  }
  finally
  {
    client.close();
  }
}
```

The `newClient()` factory method creates a new client instance with the default session timeout and default connection timeout. It takes a connection string that is a list of ZooKeeper host-port pairs and the retry policy to use.

`CuratorFramework` has a concept of a namespace. With this, it's possible to set the namespace when creating a `CuratorFramework` instance with the builder. The framework prepends the namespace to all paths when one of its APIs is called:

```
CuratorFrameworkFactory.Builder builder =
  CuratorFrameworkFactory.builder();
CuratorFramework client = builder.connectString
  (server.getConnectString()).namespace("MyApp").retryPolicy(new
  RetryOneTime(1)).build();
client.create().forPath("/test_znode", data);
```

Here, although the name of the znode is specified as `/test_znode`, the actual znode that gets created is `/MyApp/test_znode`.

The Curator framework also provides a limited-feature framework interface named `CuratorTempFramework` for temporary connections over unreliable networks, such as a WAN. In this framework, the ZooKeeper connection is closed if the session remains idle for some time.

Curator recipes

Curator provides a bunch of ready-to-use recipes for ZooKeeper. A detailed listing and description for the recipes implemented by Curator can be read from the project page at `http://curator.apache.org/curator-recipes/index.html`.

Here, we will go through brief outlines of the ZooKeeper recipes in Curator:

- **Leader election**: Curator provides two algorithms for leader election: leader latch and leader selector. Both the algorithms select a "leader" among the multiple contenders connected to the Zookeeper cluster.
  If a group of *n* participants contend for leadership with leader latch, one among the *n* participants is randomly assigned as a leader, while with leader selector, a leader is selected in the order of requests coming to the Zookeeper server. When the leader releases its leadership, another contender from the group of *n* participants in the cluster is chosen.

- **Locks**: Curator implements the following different types of distributed locks:
    - **Shared re-entrant lock**: This type of lock provides globally synchronous fully-distributed locks.
    - **Shared lock**: This is non re-entrant shared re-entrant lock.
    - **Shared re-entrant read/write lock**: This is a re-entrant read/write mutex that works across JVMs.
    - **Shared semaphore**: This is a counting semaphore that works across JVMs.
    - **Multishared lock**: This is used to manage multiple locks as a single entity. An `acquire()` call acquires all the locks. If the call fails, all the acquired paths are released. A `release()` call releases all the managed locks.

- **Barrier**: This provides implementation for both barrier and double barrier.

- **Counters**: This provides a mechanism to manage a shared integer with a shared counter. It also gives a mechanism for distributed atomic increments with distributed atomic long, distributed atomic integer, and distributed atomic value.

- **Cache**: Caching is implemented through the path cache, node cache, and tree cache recipes to keep the data of change in states of znodes, locally cached nodes and all the locally cached children of a ZK path respectively.

- **Queues**: This provides distributed queue implementation. The following different types of queues are supported:

  ◦ **Distributed queue**: This is a simple distributed queue where items put into the queue are ordered in FIFO.

  ◦ **Distributed ID queue**: This is a version of distributed queue that allows some identifiers to be associated with queue items.

  ◦ **Distributed priority queue**: This is an implementation of the distributed priority queue of ZooKeeper. Internally, it uses a distributed queue where a priority can be specified to the items.

  ◦ **Distributed delay queue**: This is a variation of the distributed priority queue that uses time as the priority. When items are added to the queue, a delay value is given. The item will not be sent to a consumer until the time elapses.

  ◦ **Simple distributed queue**: This is a replacement of the `org.apache.zookeeper.recipes.queue.DistributedQueue` queue implementation that is part of the ZooKeeper distribution.

- **Nodes**: This provides a recipe for a persistent ephemeral node; this is an ephemeral node that attempts to stay present in ZooKeeper, even with connection and session interruptions.

Curator utilities

The Curator library also provides a collection of useful utilities for ZooKeeper. Some of these are shown here:

- **Test server**: This is a local, in-process ZooKeeper server that can be used for testing

- **Test cluster**: This is an internally running ensemble of ZooKeeper servers for testing

- **ZKPaths**: This provides various static methods to use the ZooKeeper znode paths

- **EnsurePath**: This is a utility to ensure that a particular znode path is created before use

- **BlockingQueueConsumer**: This is a queue consumer similar to Java's `BlockingQueue`

- **Reaper**: This is a utility to delete paths with no children and nodes with no data

Curator extensions

The curator extension package includes extra recipes in addition to the ones included in the recipe package. The recipes in the extension package have the naming convention of `curator-x-`*name*.

The following extensions are currently available with Curator:

- **Service discovery**: This is a system to use ZooKeeper as a service discovery mechanism. We looked at a service discovery recipe using ZooKeeper in *Chapter 4, Performing Common Distributed System Tasks*.

- **Service discovery server**: This is a Curator service discovery with a REST server for for non-Java and legacy applications. It exposes RESTful web services to register, remove, and query services.

- **Curator RPC proxy**: This module implements a proxy that bridges non-Java environments with the Curator framework and recipes. It uses Apache Thrift that enables a large set of languages and environments to use Curator's capabilities and unify ZooKeeper usages across languages/environments.

- **ZKClient bridge**: This extension acts as a bridge between Curator and ZKClient (`https://github.com/sgroschupf/zkclient`). It is useful for applications written using ZKClient to use the Curator library without changing the existing code. The ZKClient bridge is not packaged as a part of the official Curator distribution. It can be found in its own package in the Maven Central repository as `curator-x-zkclient-bridge`.

So far, we have read about the Curator library and its various components. Curator implements a very nice and robust extension to the ZooKeeper APIs, abstracting away many of the complexities of ZooKeeper. It's highly recommended for developers to consider using Curator to develop distributed applications using ZooKeeper in Java language. As we have seen, the power of Curator can be harnessed from applications written in languages other than Java too.

In the next section, we will read about **Exhibitor**, which is a tool for the management of ZooKeeper server processes.

Exhibitor

Exhibitor is a supervisor service to manage ZooKeeper server instances. Developed and open sourced by Netflix, Exhibitor is very useful for ZooKeeper instance monitoring, backup/recovery, cleanup, and visualization.

 The Netflix Exhibitor home page is located at `https://github.com/Netflix/exhibitor`.

Managing and administering a ZooKeeper cluster requires a lot of manual effort, which might lead to human errors and create undesirable problems in the applications. A ZooKeeper ensemble is statically configured with the configuration of each individual instance comprising a configuration file. This file must be identical on each of the ZooKeeper instances. The reconfiguration of the ensemble requires an update of this configuration file as well as a restart of the server process. A proper configuration is essential for correct functioning of ZooKeeper. Along with the right configuration needs, ZooKeeper might also need a periodic backup of the transaction logs, cleanup of the logs, and so on.

Exhibitor provides all the preceding ZooKeeper management needs along with a lot of other features, which are cited as follows:

- **Monitoring**: Exhibitor monitors the ZooKeeper server. If the ZooKeeper server process crashes or is not running for some reasons, Exhibitor rewrites the configuration file and restarts the server process.

- **Log cleanup**: Exhibitor can periodically do a cleanup of ZooKeeper logs. However, post version 3.4.x, ZooKeeper comes with an option to auto purge the logfile.

- **Backup/restore**: Exhibitor can be used to back up the ZooKeeper transaction logfile. It also allows indexing of these logs by which any specified transactions can be searched and used to restore a given znode to the ZooKeeper instance.

- **Cluster-wide configuration**: Exhibitor enables the application of configuration changes to the entire ZooKeeper ensemble by presenting a single system view.

- **Rolling configuration update**: Exhibitor allows hot updating of configuration; this allows configuration updates to be done even when the ZooKeeper ensemble is running, without any downtime.

- **REST API**: Exhibitor exposes a REST API that allows developers to write programs to carry out ZooKeeper management tasks.

- **Visualization**: Exhibitor presents a graphical visualization of the ZooKeeper tree.

- **Curator integration**: Exhibitor and Curator can be configured to work together. It allows Curator instances to get updated for any changes made to the ZooKeeper ensemble.

 More details on this integration can be found at `http://curator.apache.org/exhibitor.html`.

Exhibitor binaries are available from the Maven Central repository. They come in two versions:

- **Standalone**: This version provides a preconfigured, self-contained Jetty-based application. Details on running the standalone application can be found at `https://github.com/Netflix/exhibitor/wiki/Running-Exhibitor`.

- **Core**: This version allows us to build extensions to Exhibitor by integrating with the existing application.

Summary

In this chapter, you learned about Apache Curator, which is a high-level wrapper library and framework for Apache ZooKeeper. Curator makes programming with ZooKeeper very simple by abstracting many of the intricacies and also extends it by providing a lot of add-on features and recipes. Curator also makes it possible for legacy applications to use ZooKeeper's capabilities through various extensions. We also looked at Exhibitor to supervise ZooKeeper server instances, and you learned how it can be used for easy configuration of the ZooKeeper ensemble and many other maintenance tasks.

By now, we have almost come to the end of learning the essentials of ZooKeeper. In the next chapter, we will look at how ZooKeeper is being used in other software projects, and we will also look at the tools used to achieve distributed coordination. We will also look at a few examples of how ZooKeeper is used by organizations on their production platforms. This will give you a feel that what you learned throughout this book is actually being used in real-world applications.

7
ZooKeeper in Action

In the last six chapters, we learned all the essentials about Apache ZooKeeper, which has given us a firm grip on its background concepts, usage, and administration. We read about community projects such as Curator, which makes programming with ZooKeeper much simpler, and also adds more functionality on top of it. We saw how Exhibitor makes the managing of ZooKeeper instances easier in a production environment. ZooKeeper is one of the successful projects from Apache Software Foundation, and has gained wide adoption by other projects and organizations in their production platforms.

In this chapter, we are going to read about how ZooKeeper is used by software projects for their inherent need of distributed coordination. We will particularly look at the following projects that use and depend on ZooKeeper for some of their functionality:

- Apache BookKeeper
- Apache Hadoop
- Apache HBase
- Apache Helix
- OpenStack Nova

We will also look at how ZooKeeper is used by organizations such as Yahoo!, Netflix, Facebook, Twitter, eBay, and so on in their production platform to achieve distributed coordination and synchronization. In addition to this, we will also learn how companies such as Nutanix and VMware leverage ZooKeeper in their enterprise-grade compute and storage appliances.

 The use of ZooKeeper by various organizations has been compiled from blogs and tech notes available in the public domain. The author or the publisher of this book bears no responsibility for the authenticity of the information.

Projects powered by ZooKeeper

In this section, we will delve into the details of how various open source software projects use Apache ZooKeeper to implement some of their functionality. As it's beyond the scope of this book to give a full functional description of the individual projects, readers are advised to go through the respective project pages to learn more about their design and architectural details.

Apache BookKeeper

The Apache BookKeeper (`http://zookeeper.apache.org/bookkeeper/`) is a subproject of ZooKeeper. BookKeeper is a highly available and reliable distributed logging service. Hedwig is a topic-based distributed publish/subscribe system built on BookKeeper. In this section, we will take a sneak peek of Apache BookKeeper.

BookKeeper can be used to reliably log streams of records. It achieves high availability through replication. Applications that need to log operations or transactions in a reliable fashion so that crash recovery can be done in case of failure can use BookKeeper. It is highly scalable, fault-tolerant, and high performant. In a nutshell, BookKeeper comprises the following components:

- **Ledger**: Ledgers are streams of logs that consist of a sequence of bytes. Log streams are written sequentially to a ledger in an append-only semantics. It uses the **write-ahead logging (WAL)** protocol.

- **BookKeeper client**: A BookKeeper client creates ledgers. It runs in the same machine as the application and enables the application to write to the ledgers.

- **Bookie**: Bookies are BookKeeper storage servers that store and manage the ledgers.

- **Metadata storage service**: The information related to ledgers and bookies are stored with this service.

BookKeeper uses ZooKeeper for its metadata storage service. Whenever the application creates a ledger with the BookKeeper client, it stores the metadata about the ledger in the metadata storage service backed by a ZooKeeper instance. Clients use ZooKeeper coordination to ascertain that only a single client is writing to a ledger. The writer has to close the ledger before any other client issues a read operation on that ledger. BookKeeper ensures that after the ledger has been closed, other clients can see the same content while reading from it. The closing of a ledger is done by creating a close znode for the ledger, and the use of ZooKeeper prevents any race conditions.

Apache Hadoop

The Apache Hadoop project (http://hadoop.apache.org/) is an umbrella of projects, and ZooKeeper is one of the allied subprojects.

Apache Hadoop is a distributed framework that processes large datasets using clusters that span over a large number of nodes. It uses simple programming models such as MapReduce to process the datasets. It is scalable up to thousands of servers. Rather than rely on hardware to deliver high availability, the library itself is designed to detect and handle failures at the application layer.

The project includes the following components:

- **Hadoop Common**: This includes the libraries and utilities used by other Hadoop modules

- **Hadoop Distributed File System (HDFS)**: This is a scalable and fault-tolerant distributed filesystem that stores large datasets and provides high-performant access to it

- **Hadoop YARN (Yet Another Resource Negotiator)**: YARN is a distributed framework that provides job scheduling and cluster resource management

- **Hadoop MapReduce**: This is a YARN-based software framework that performs parallel processing of large datasets

Apache ZooKeeper is used in Hadoop to implement high availability in YARN and HDFS.

YARN (http://bit.ly/1xDJG8r) is the next-generation compute and resource-management framework in Apache Hadoop. It consists of a global **ResourceManager (RM)** and a per-application ApplicationMaster:

- The RM mediates resource allocation among all the applications in the system. It has two components: Scheduler and ApplicationsManager. The Scheduler is responsible for allocating resources to the applications, and the ApplicationsManager manages job- and application-specific details. RM uses a per-node daemon called the NodeManager to monitor resource usage (CPU, memory, disk, and network) and report the same to the RM.

- The ApplicationMaster is a library that is specific to every application. It runs along with the application in the Hadoop cluster, does resource negotiating with the RM, and assists the NodeManager(s) to execute and monitor the tasks.

The RM coordinates the running tasks in a YARN cluster. However, in a Hadoop cluster, only one instance of the RM runs and is a single point of failure. A ZooKeeper solution provides **high availability (HA)** to the RM, which allows a failover of the RM to another machine when the active one crashes.

The solution works by storing the current internal state of the RM in ZooKeeper. Since ZooKeeper itself is a highly available data store for small amount of data, it makes the RM state highly available too. Whenever an RM resumes after a restart or a crash, it loads the internal state from ZooKeeper.

An extension to the solution to provide failover capability is to have multiple RMs, of which one is in an active role and the others are mere standbys. When the active RM goes down, a leader election can be done with ZooKeeper to elect a new RM. Use of ZooKeeper prevents the potential problem of more than one node claiming the active role (fencing).

 More details on **YARN HA** with ZooKeeper can be found on the blog written by Karthik Kambatla, Wing Yew Poon, and Vikram Srivastava at `http://blog.cloudera.com/blog/2014/05/how-apache-hadoop-yarn-ha-works/`.

ZooKeeper is also used in Hadoop for the purpose of achieving high availability for HDFS. The metadata node or the **NameNode (NN)**, which stores the metadata information of the whole filesystem is a **single point of failure (SPOF)** in HDFS. The NN being a SPOF was a problem till Hadoop 1.x. However, in Hadoop 2.x, an automatic failover mechanism is available in HDFS, for a fast failover of the NN role from the active node to another node in the event of a crash.

The problem is solved in a similar manner to the approach used for YARN RM. Multiple NNs are set up, of which only one NN assumes the active role, and the others remain in the standby mode. All client filesystem operations go to the active NN in the cluster, while the standby acts as a slave. The standby NN maintains enough state about the filesystem namespace to provide a fast failover. Each of the NNs (active as well as standbys) runs a **ZKFailoverController (ZKFC)** in it. ZKFC maintains a heartbeat with the ZooKeeper service. The ZKFC in the active NN holds a special "lock" znode through an ephemeral znode in the ZooKeeper tree. In the event of a failure of the current active NN, the session with the ZooKeeper service expires, triggering an election for the next active NN. One among the standby NNs wins the election and acquires the active NN role.

Apache HBase

Apache HBase (`http://hbase.apache.org/`) is a distributed, scalable, big data store. It's a non-relational database on top of HDFS.

In HBase architecture, there is a master server called HMaster, and a number of slave servers called RegionServer. The HMaster monitors the RegionServers, which store and manage the regions. Regions are contiguous ranges of rows stored together. The data is stored in persistent storage files called HFiles.

HBase uses ZooKeeper for distributed coordination. Every RegionServer creates its own ephemeral znode in ZooKeeper, which the HMaster uses in order to discover available servers. HBase also uses ZooKeeper to ensure that there is only one HMaster running and to store the root of the regions for region discovery. ZooKeeper is an essential component in HBase, without which HBase can't operate.

> For more details on HBase architecture, refer to `http://hbase.apache.org/book.html`.

Apache Helix

Apache Helix (`http://helix.apache.org/`) is a cluster management framework. It provides a generic way of automatically managing the resources in a cluster. Helix acts as a decision subsystem for the cluster, and is responsible for the following tasks and many more:

- Automating the reassignment of resources to the nodes
- Handling node failure detection and recovery
- Dynamic cluster reconfiguration (node and resource addition/deletion)
- Scheduling of maintenance tasks (backups, index rebuilds, and so on)
- Maintaining load balancing and flow control in the cluster

In order to store the current cluster state, Helix needs a distributed and highly available configuration or cluster metadata store, for which it uses ZooKeeper.

ZooKeeper provides Helix with the following capabilities:

- This framework represents the PERSISTENT state, which remains until it's removed
- This framework also represents the TRANSIENT/EPHEMERAL state, which goes away when the process that created the state leaves the cluster

- This framework notifies the subsystem when there is a change in the PERSISTENT and EPHEMERAL state of the cluster

Helix also allows simple lookups of task assignments through the configuration store built on top of ZooKeeper. Through this, clients can look up where the tasks are currently assigned. This way, Helix can also provide a service discovery registry.

OpenStack Nova

OpenStack (`http://www.openstack.org/`) is an open source software stack for the creation and management of private and public clouds. It is designed to manage pools of compute, storage, and networking resources in data centers, allowing the management of these resources through a consolidated dashboard and flexible APIs.

Nova is the software component in OpenStack, which is responsible for managing the compute resources, where **virtual machines (VMs)** are hosted in a cloud computing environment. It is also known as the OpenStack Compute Service. OpenStack Nova provides a cloud computing fabric controller, supporting a wide variety of virtualization technologies such as KVM, Xen, VMware, and many more. In addition to its native API, it also includes compatibility with Amazon EC2 and S3 APIs.

Nova depends on up-to-date information about the availability of the various compute nodes and services that run on them, for its proper operation. For example, the virtual machine placement operation requires to know the currently available compute nodes and their current state.

Nova uses ZooKeeper to implement an efficient membership service, which monitors the availability of registered services. This is done through the ZooKeeper ServiceGroup Driver, which works by using ZooKeeper's ephemeral znodes. Each service registers by creating an ephemeral znode on startup. Now, when the service dies, ZooKeeper will automatically delete the corresponding ephemeral znode. The removal of this znode can be used to trigger the corresponding recovery logic.

For example, when a compute node crashes, the nova-compute service that is running in that node also dies. This causes the session with ZooKeeper service to expire, and as a result, ZooKeeper deletes the ephemeral znode created by the nova-compute service. If the cloud controller keeps a watch on this node-deletion event, it will come to know about the compute node crash and can trigger a migration procedure to evacuate all the VMs that are running in the failed compute node to other nodes. This way, high availability of the VMs can be ensured in real time.

ZooKeeper is also being considered for the following use cases in OpenStack Nova:

- Storing the configuration metadata (`nova.conf`)
- Maintaining high availability of services and automatic failover using leader election

Organizations powered by ZooKeeper

In this section, we will learn about how organizations around the world are using Apache ZooKeeper in their production clusters to solve distributed coordination problems. The real-world use cases depicted here give us a transparent view of how ZooKeeper can be an indispensable component for distributed platforms. The following organizations use Apache ZooKeeper:

Yahoo!

ZooKeeper was originally developed by Yahoo! before it became an Apache project. It is used for a multitude of services inside Yahoo! to perform leader election, configuration management, naming system, sharding, distributed locking, group membership, and so on. Yahoo! is a big Hadoop shop that performs analysis in its massive datasets, and ZooKeeper is used for various distributed coordination and synchronization tasks.

Facebook

Facebook uses ZooKeeper in its messaging platform and many other use cases. Facebook's messaging system is powered by a system called cell system. The entire messaging system (e-mail, SMS, Facebook Chat, and the Facebook Inbox) is divided into cells. Cells are composed of a cluster of servers and services, and each cell serves only a fraction of Facebook users. The use of cells has the following advantages:

- Incremental scaling with minuscule failures
- Easy upgrading of hardware and software
- Failures affect only the cell boundary, which affects limited users
- Hosting cells in distributed data centers avoids disasters

Each cell comprises a cluster of servers and is coordinated by a ZooKeeper ensemble. The servers that host a particular application register themselves with ZooKeeper. The mapping between users and servers is then done using the consistent hashing algorithm. Basically, the nodes are arranged in a ring, and each node is responsible for a specified range of the users depending on the hash values.

If a node fails, another node in the neighboring position in the ring takes over the load for those users affected by the failure. This allows for an even distribution of the load and also enables easy addition and removal of nodes into and from the cluster in the cell.

eBay

eBay uses ZooKeeper to develop a job type limiter. The job limiter limits the execution of the same type of jobs from running simultaneously beyond a specified number in the grid. For each job type, the type limiter keeps track of the running count and the limit. When the running count hits the limit, spawning of a new job is not allowed until a job of that type finishes or terminates. This job type limiter is used for jobs that use third-party services using APIs to update the maximum bid for keyword ads. Usually, the API call capacity is limited. Even if the grid has enough capacity to run hundreds of jobs, the job limiter system built with ZooKeeper allows only a predetermined number (for example, N) of concurrent jobs against a partner API. The type limiter ensures that the $(N+1)^{th}$ job waits until one of the N running jobs has completed.

 For details on how the job type limiter system is implemented, visit the blog *Grid Computing with Fault-Tolerant Actors and ZooKeeper* by *Matthias Spycher* at `http://bit.ly/11eyJ1b`.

Twitter

Twitter uses ZooKeeper service discovery within its data centers. Services register themselves in ZooKeeper to advertise the services for clients. This allows clients to know what services are currently available and the servers where these are hosted. Clients can also query for services in the service discovery system. The system ensures an up-to-date host list that provides the queried services and makes it available for the clients. Whenever new capacity is added for the services, the client will automatically become aware of it and can do load balancing across all servers.

Netflix

Netflix is an avid ZooKeeper user in its distributed platform, which led them to develop Curator and Exhibitor to enhance the functionalities of ZooKeeper. A few of the use cases of ZooKeeper/Curator at Netflix are as follows:

- Ensuring the generation of unique values in various sequence ID generators
- Cassandra backups

- Implementing the TrackID service
- Performing leader election with ZooKeeper for various distributed tasks
- Implementing a distributed semaphore for concurrent jobs
- Distributed caching

Zynga

Zynga uses ZooKeeper for configuration management of their hosted games. ZooKeeper allows Zynga to update the configuration files for a plethora of online games, which are used across the world by millions of users in a very short span of time. The games are served from Zynga's multiple data centers. With ZooKeeper, the configuration's system updates thousands of configuration files in a very small span of time. The configurations are validated by validation systems against the business logic to ensure that configurations are updated correctly and services are properly configured to the updated data. In the absence of ZooKeeper, the configuration update at the same time in a short time interval would be a real nightmare. Again, failure to sync these configuration files within the available time span would have caused severe service disruption.

Nutanix

Nutanix (http://www.nutanix.com/) develops a hyper-converged storage and compute solution, which leverages local components of a host machine, such as storage capacity (disks) and compute (CPUs), to create a distributed platform for virtualization. This solution is known as the Nutanix Virtual Computing Platform. It supports industry-standard hypervisor ESXi, KVM, and Hyper-V. The platform is bundled in the appliance form factor with two nodes or four nodes. A VM in the platform known as the Nutanix Controller VM works as the decision subsystem, which manages the platform.

The Nutanix platform uses Apache ZooKeeper as a Cluster configuration manager. The configuration data that pertains to the platform, such as hostnames, IP addresses, and the cluster state, is stored in a ZooKeeper ensemble. ZooKeeper is also used to query the state of the various services that run in the platform.

 More details on Nutanix architecture are available on the website by *Steven Poitras* at http://stevenpoitras.com/the-nutanix-bible/

VMware vSphere Storage Appliance

VMware **vSphere Storage Appliance (VSA)** is a software-storage appliance. The VMware VSA comes in a cluster configuration of two or three nodes, known as the VSA Storage Cluster. A virtual machine instance inside each of the VMware ESXiTM host in the VSA Storage Cluster claims all the available local directed attached storage space and presents it as one mirrored volume of all the ESXi hosts in the VMware vCenter Server datacenter. It uses the NFS protocol to export the volume.

VSA uses ZooKeeper as the base clustering library for the following primitives:

- As a cluster membership model to detect VSA failures in the cluster
- As a distributed metadata storage system to store the cluster states
- As a leader elector to select a master VSA that performs metadata operations

 More details on VMware VSA can be found in the technical paper *VMware vSphere Storage Appliance Deep Dive* by *Cormac Hogan* at http://vmw.re/1uzUaFN

Summary

In this chapter, we got acquainted with how ZooKeeper runs as a core component inside many software systems for providing distributed coordination and synchronization. We saw how the data and API model of ZooKeeper along with the recipes help other software systems to achieve their functionality. We also read about the usage of ZooKeeper by many big organizations in their production clusters.

Finally, we have reached the end of this wonderful journey of reading and learning the essentials about Apache ZooKeeper. I believe that by now, you have attained a firm grasp over the various topics on ZooKeeper, which we discussed so far in this book. Apache ZooKeeper is a mature software project, yet it is evolving everyday due to wide adoption and community traction. You are advised to follow the project to find out more about the enhancements and new features that are added to it from time to time. Also, it is recommended that you participate in the ZooKeeper project by subscribing to the developer mailing list, contributing bug fixes, and submitting new feature requests.

The following link cites the details on how to contribute to Apache ZooKeeper:

https://cwiki.apache.org/confluence/display/ZOOKEEPER/HowToContribute

Index

Thank you for buying
Apache ZooKeeper Essentials

About Packt Publishing

Packt, pronounced 'packed', published its first book, *Mastering phpMyAdmin for Effective MySQL Management*, in April 2004, and subsequently continued to specialize in publishing highly focused books on specific technologies and solutions.

Our books and publications share the experiences of your fellow IT professionals in adapting and customizing today's systems, applications, and frameworks. Our solution-based books give you the knowledge and power to customize the software and technologies you're using to get the job done. Packt books are more specific and less general than the IT books you have seen in the past. Our unique business model allows us to bring you more focused information, giving you more of what you need to know, and less of what you don't.

Packt is a modern yet unique publishing company that focuses on producing quality, cutting-edge books for communities of developers, administrators, and newbies alike. For more information, please visit our website at www.packtpub.com.

About Packt Open Source

In 2010, Packt launched two new brands, Packt Open Source and Packt Enterprise, in order to continue its focus on specialization. This book is part of the Packt Open Source brand, home to books published on software built around open source licenses, and offering information to anybody from advanced developers to budding web designers. The Open Source brand also runs Packt's Open Source Royalty Scheme, by which Packt gives a royalty to each open source project about whose software a book is sold.

Writing for Packt

We welcome all inquiries from people who are interested in authoring. Book proposals should be sent to author@packtpub.com. If your book idea is still at an early stage and you would like to discuss it first before writing a formal book proposal, then please contact us; one of our commissioning editors will get in touch with you.

We're not just looking for published authors; if you have strong technical skills but no writing experience, our experienced editors can help you develop a writing career, or simply get some additional reward for your expertise.

[PACKT] PUBLISHING

open source*
community experience distilled

Learning Storm

ISBN: 978-1-78398-132-8   Paperback: 252 pages

Create real-time stream processing applications with Apache Storm

1. Integrate Storm with other Big Data technologies like Hadoop, HBase, and Apache Kafka.

2. Explore log processing and machine learning using Storm.

3. Step-by-step and easy-to-understand guide to effortlessly create applications with Storm.

Apache Solr High Performance

ISBN: 978-1-78216-482-1   Paperback: 124 pages

Boost the performance of Solr instances and troubleshoot real-time problems

1. Achieve high scores by boosting query time and index time, implementing boost queries and functions using the Dismax query parser and formulae.

2. Set up and use SolrCloud for distributed indexing and searching, and implement distributed search using Shards.

3. Use GeoSpatial search, handling homophones, and ignoring listed words from being indexed and searched.

Please check **www.PacktPub.com** for information on our titles

Apache Accumulo for Developers

ISBN: 978-1-78328-599-0   Paperback: 120 pages

Build and integrate Accumulo clusters with various cloud platforms

1. Shows you how to build Accumulo, Hadoop, and ZooKeeper clusters from scratch on both Windows and Linux.

2. Allows you to get hands-on knowledge about how to run Accumulo on Amazon EC2, Google Cloud Platform, Rackspace, and Windows Azure Cloud platforms.

3. Packed with practical examples to enable you to manipulate Accumulo with ease.

Scaling Big Data with Hadoop and Solr

ISBN: 978-1-78328-137-4   Paperback: 144 pages

Learn exciting new ways to build efficient, high performance enterprise search repositories for Big Data using Hadoop and Solr

1. Understand the different approaches of making Solr work on Big Data as well as the benefits and drawbacks.

2. Learn from interesting, real-life use cases for Big Data search along with sample code.

3. Work with the Distributed Enterprise Search without prior knowledge of Hadoop and Solr.

Please check **www.PacktPub.com** for information on our titles

www.ingramcontent.com/pod-product-compliance
Lightning Source LLC
Chambersburg PA
CBHW060138060326

40690CB00018B/3923

* 9 7 8 1 7 8 4 3 9 1 3 2 4 *